Dentistry Customer Service Superstars

Six attitudes that bring out our best

By: Cary Cavitt
Author, Speaker and Founder of
Service Starts With a Smile™
Visit us at: www.carycavitt.com

Copyright © 2017 by Cary Cavitt

All Rights Reserved

ISBN: 9781542344708

Attitude: at·ti·tude
A way of thinking or behaving.

Table of Contents

	Introduction	1
Chapter 1	Sara the Dentistry Customer Service Superstar	9
Chapter 2	The Attitude of Friendliness	13
Chapter 3	The Attitude of Enthusiasm	31
Chapter 4	The Attitude of Caring	45
Chapter 5	The Attitude of Respect	61
Chapter 6	The Attitude of Encouraging	81
Chapter 7	The Attitude of Thankfulness	95
Chapter 8	When Attitudes Go Astray	107
Chapter 9	A Time to Improve	113
Chapter 10	Closing Thoughts	127
	About the Author	129

"The only real handicap in life
is a bad attitude."

Introduction

Dentistry Customer Service Superstars
Six attitudes that bring out our best

"Every successful organization does not live solely from a business point of view. It also lives with the heart in mind."

It has been said that attitude is everything when it comes to approaching the many challenges in life. How we view each day can be a reflection of the attitude that we carry with us. We can choose either to look at every situation with an attitude that will help or hinder us. It is our choice alone.

In the area of dentistry customer service it is no different. How we treat each customer is a reflection of the attitude that we bring with us to the job. Our attitude can assist or hold us back in providing the best possible service. That is why it is essential to understand that certain attitudes can make us dentistry customer service superstars if we will only learn to apply them into our lives.

Over the years I have found it quite fascinating how our inner attitudes can determine so much of how we view daily life. This is especially true in the area of serving customers. We can have all of the right training in how to treat others, but it will never quite work if we do not have the six attitudes that I will be discussing in each chapter.

DENTISTRY CUSTOMER SERVICE SUPERSTARS

Since each of us can relate to what it feels like to be a customer, we will discover throughout the pages that the great memories we have personally had of being served well were in reality the result of being assisted by someone who had these qualities. On the other hand, we can all relate to moments as a customer where we were treated rather poorly. This too can be tied in with being served by someone who simply lacked these six attitudes.

A famous 20th century writer once penned…

> *I have learned silence from the talkative, toleration from the intolerant, and kindness from the unkind, yet strange, I am ungrateful to those teachers.*

Over the past 30 years I have personally served over 100,000 customers. And like you, I have played the role of a customer in literally hundreds of different situations. Think of the countless experiences that we have all had of being a customer and the service that was provided to us. Here are just a few examples in the past year alone where I have played the role of a customer:

At a grocery store.
At a barber shop.
At a presentation.
At a bank.
At a dentist office.
At a restaurant.
At a retail store.
At a golf club.
At an airport.
At a resort.
…And hundreds of other organizations.

I am sure that you can also think of pleasant and not so pleasant experiences that have occurred this past year as a customer. I am always amazed when talking to friends about the topic of customer service in the marketplace. Without hesitation, I am then given a war

Introduction

story about an episode that had recently happened to my friend and how disappointing the experience was. My first thought is that the person serving my friend did not have the right attitude. This alone would have made a total difference in the perception of the service provided. The person serving may have gone through company training and read the policy manual for the particular job but did not understand the most important part of service. This of course is projecting to the customer the six attitudes that we will be looking at.

There is less to fear from outside competition than from inside inefficiency, discourtesy, and bad service.

In the final analysis, it really just comes down to having the right attitudes on and off the job. This alone can make all of the difference in how well we treat every person we come in contact with. This book is intended to focus on these six attitudes that will positively change the way we care for others.

Let's briefly look at these attitudes and how they affect the perception that others will have of our service:

The Attitude of Friendliness

Customers first and foremost measure our service by the friendliness shown.

The first chapter will look at the attitude of friendliness. Without question, this attitude must be consistently present when serving our customers. When friendliness is lacking, customers will soon find another place to do business with.

The Attitude of Enthusiasm

Serving with enthusiasm adds to the customer's experience.

The attitude of enthusiasm will be our focus in the second chapter. Our customers will quickly take notice when we serve with enthusiasm. Because today's consumer is looking for an experience, our enthusiasm will only enhance their excitement in the product or service being provided.

The Attitude of Caring

Loyalty occurs when customers sense that we genuinely care.

The third chapter will focus on the attitude of caring. Of all six attitudes I would rate this attitude at the top simply because caring is at the heart of five-star dentistry customer service. Our customers will sense when we are genuine and earnestly care about their needs more than simply attempting to make a sale. This attitude also will determine customer loyalty in the future.

The Attitude of Respect

Showing respect demonstrates our willingness to serve others.

The fourth chapter we will look at the attitude of respect. We affirm and give a person value when we show respect. This attitude will play a pivotal point in retaining customers. The other benefit of continually showing respect is that it is returned back to us. This also is true with every other attitude that we will be discussing throughout the following pages.

The Attitude of Encouraging

Encouragement creates a positive environment for both the customer and company.

INTRODUCTION

The attitude of encouraging will be discussed in the fifth chapter. This attitude has many benefits not only to our customers but also to our co-workers. Every person is positively changed when they encounter people who encourage. This is especially true with those we work with. This attitude will play a key role in how well we build our dentistry customer service team.

The Attitude of Thankfulness

Customers who feel appreciated will rate our service higher.

The last chapter will focus on the attitude of thankfulness. *Customers cannot help but see our service as excellent when we sincerely appreciate their business.* This little attitude is powerful when it comes to serving others. This is because we all like to be appreciated and can tell when we have been served by someone who has a heart of gratitude.

My goal is to write a book that is quick to read and gets to the point of how each attitude will determine our ability to provide outstanding service. The other vision that I have for *Dentistry Customer Service Superstars* is that it will be given to those who are on the front lines everyday with customers. It is my goal that this book will give readers a better understanding of the appropriate attitudes that will not only improve lives, but also assist in serving others in a more enjoyable manner.

I once read a quote that has never left me. It simply said:

"People can just about forgive anything except the way that another person made them feel."

Dentistry customer service Superstars

I am convinced that the key to providing five-star dentistry customer service is to treat people with these six attitudes. Dentistry customer service is simply about meeting the needs of another person in a warm and friendly manner. In reality it has very little to do with policies, manuals, rules and regulations. Great dentistry customer service is simply caring about others.

> *The greatest virtues are those that are most useful to other persons.*
> *--Aristotle*

The intelligent organizations always remember that every business transaction is about people helping other people meet a need. Our customers are really not asking for much. They just would like to be served in a friendly and helpful manner. This will happen when we begin to understand that it must start with the right attitude…six to be exact.

Best regards,
Cary Cavitt
Founder and Speaker of
Service That Attracts Seminars ™
www.carycavittconsulting.com

This book is dedicated to those throughout my life who have shown by their example how the right attitude can make all the difference.

Chapter 1

Sara the Dentistry Customer Service Superstar

There was something distinctively different and attractive in the way that Sara Smith treated others. As an employee, she was a shining example for other co-workers simply because of her friendly personality. People tended to gravitate toward her. This was especially true in her relationships with the many loyal customers that she had won over the years. *Sara had what it took to be what I would classify as a dentistry customer service superstar.* She had a way of bringing customers back and encouraging other co-workers to achieve their best. Sara was an excellent example to others and made a positive impact at her organization.

One feature that Sara consistently showed to other people was her genuine friendliness. She had a way of making co-workers and customers feel welcomed simply by the way that she treated them. Her friendly smile and pleasant tone of voice made others feel comfortable from the start. People also were attracted to the way that she genuinely took an interest in them. She could instantly drop everything she was doing and give another person her undivided attention. The way Sara intently listened without interrupting made others feel that she really cared about them and understood what they were saying. It was evident within the first few minutes of being around Sara that she sincerely cared about people.

Another admirable trait that defined Sara was her undying enthusiasm for life. She lived in such a way that made others want what she had.

It was as if Sara looked at each day as a gift to be treasured. It would be evident after being around her for a short time that she appreciated life. The enthusiasm for living also affected others who were around her. Never one to complain, Sara had a way of making others feel appreciated. *Customers who were helped by her would walk away feeling that they were served by the most thankful person in the world.* This not only left them with a great feeling as they walked out the door, but also made them want to return simply because of Sara and the way she made them feel.

Because of Sara's non-critical attitude, she always made others feel accepted. Always one to show respect, Sara had a way of bringing people up. Her encouraging words to co-workers and customers were heartfelt. Never one to use empty flattery, Sara was never afraid to compliment another person. She was never heard complaining or gossiping. Her words were always helpful and encouraging. Never once did she criticize or use inappropriate language.

Her sincerity in helping as well as expressing appreciation to her customers had a way of bringing them back time and again. She was valued by her organization, encouraging to her co-workers, and treasured by her customers. *This is what made Sara a dentistry customer service superstar.*

♥

The Attitude of

Friendliness

Friendly, polite, cordial, hospitable, neighborly, hearty, warmhearted, familiar, on good terms, welcoming.

Chapter 2

The Attitude of Friendliness

*Customers first and foremost measure our service
by the friendliness shown.*

What word in the American language is more attractive than friendliness? The word itself makes us want to come closer. Ever since we have taken our first steps as a small child we have been attracted to those who are kind to us. This is one attitude that wins every time. People from all walks of life and every corner of the world appreciate when someone is nice to them.

I call this allure *the friendly factor*. In regards to the business world, most customers typically expect average run-of-the-mill service. They do not anticipate much in the area of sincere friendliness. Maybe it's because of our fast paced world and the busyness of life that make us forget to slow down just long enough to show someone some kindness.

When we are on the other side of the counter and play the role of a customer, we also expect the service to be somewhat average. *But when we encounter a person who is sincerely friendly to us we automatically feel that the service is wonderful!* This is because genuine friendliness is seldom expected in the marketplace. This little attitude will also give our customers a reason to tell others about the great service that we provide.

Why is friendliness so appealing? I believe that every human being is attracted to people who are kindhearted. Think of those in the past who were friendly to us for no apparent reason. In these memorable situations we may silently wonder why this person was so kind. In some cases we may even question the motive and secretly speculate if they are after something. The reason that we may be unsure about someone showing us kindness is because it usually happens so infrequently in our daily lives. But when we encounter someone who is genuinely friendly to us, there is something deep inside that wants to welcome it with open arms. Even though we may be uncertain at first to another's genuine kindheartedness, in the end we all respond positively to these memorable moments.

As those who serve customers, we have the perfect occasion to show goodwill to others. It gives us a great opportunity to be friendly. *I believe this attitude alone can change an entire organization if people simply understood the powerful attraction that kindness brings.* If an individual were to focus on being friendlier to others, he or she would instantly notice others going out of their way to be kind in return.

I am always puzzled when doing business with a company that lacks in this area. The first thought that comes to mind is why any organization would put employees out in front who project an unfriendly attitude toward others. This not only makes customers feel uncomfortable, but also gives them a legitimate reason not to return in the future. I have witnessed this countless times in playing the role of a customer. It made me want to depart as soon as possible. This of course is not a good thing for business.

Wherever there is a human being, there is an opportunity for kindness.
—Seneca

On the other hand I have had situations where a service representative has treated me with such consideration that I left feeling overwhelmed by the kindness shown. *This left an indelible impression that the service was outstanding.* When I look back at those pleasant experiences I can now see that it was nothing more than one person showing kindness to another person. *The perception that I had of the service provided was enhanced simply because someone showed some unexpected friendliness.*

Chapter 2

I am convinced that if more dentistry customer service representatives projected a little more kindness to each customer, the customer would walk away feeling that the service was outstanding. Why do I say this? Because customers as a whole do not expect it! I believe that customers always appreciate when unanticipated kindness is shown to them. This truth is universal. *In every business transaction, whether it is selling a product or providing a service, the customer is judging our service on the basis of whether or not we are serving them with an attitude of friendliness.*

Let's look at an example of how friendliness plays a key role in projecting a first impression for the customer. Think about the restaurant business. The first contact made when stepping through the door is a greeting by someone who will seat us. This person will play a major role in how we feel about the restaurant. If the greeter is inattentive and hurried we may make a poor judgment about the overall service of the restaurant. If the greeter starts with a warm welcome and friendly smile, we automatically feel that the experience will be pleasant.

How can we be friendlier?

Don't wait for people to be friendly.
Show them how.

I hope by now we can see how the attitude of friendliness plays a major role in how customers perceive our operation. But just knowing that this attitude is important in dentistry customer service is not enough. We can become convinced that showing kindness to our customers is essential in building a great service team, but still fail if we do not actually project it in our daily contact with customers. The goal is to learn some important guidelines that will help us become more considerate.

Having wisdom is knowing what to do next.
Having virtue is actually doing it.

The first guiding principle in providing great dentistry customer service is to realize that our job is to simply meet the requests of the customer. We are given the job of taking care of whatever need the customer may have at the moment. Since this is the first commandment of dentistry customer service, it seems only logical that we would want the service to be as pleasant as possible. If we understand that our job is to meet the customer's needs, our attitude should be as friendly as possible in order to make the overall experience wonderful.

The second guiding principle in learning to be friendlier is to ask ourselves how we like to be treated when we take on the role as a customer. I am convinced that 100% of us would declare that we would want to be treated in a friendly manner. This alone should convince us of the importance of how we should treat others. The age-old saying that we should treat others the way that we would like to be treated is true in every facet of life, including serving our customers.

Kindness, like a boomerang, always returns.

Learning to be friendly takes practice. I once read a wise saying that said you learn to be kind by being kind. I would agree with this. Being friendly to others may come easy to some people, but that does not mean that everyone cannot improve in this department. The goal is to take small steps in showing kindness each day. Start off by greeting your customers with a smile and a more pleasant tone of voice. Learn to be more attentive and have the mindset that you are there for them. Others will quickly notice these little gestures. Soon you will begin to treat more and more people with genuine friendliness without even noticing that you are doing it. They in turn will begin to treat you in a more pleasant manner simply as a token of their appreciation in response to your unexpected kindness.

Twelve benefits of friendliness

"No act of kindness, no matter how small, is ever wasted."

CHAPTER 2

- Aesop, Greek fabulist (6th century B.C.)

Being a friendly person has multiple benefits not only in serving customers, but also in daily life. Having a friendly attitude makes our journey much smoother. Here are twelve additional advantages that friendliness brings both on and off the job:

1. Friendly people know how to have fun

Friendly people are much more inclined to have fun. On the other hand, unfriendly people seem to seldom enjoy the gift of life. *Have you ever met someone who had a tendency of being unfriendly who also knew how to have fun?* These two seldom go together. In terms of dentistry customer service, fun is the name of the game in much of today's business economy. We live in a world where fun and entertainment are the themes of a vast majority of organizations. Customers today are looking for more than just a hamburger and fries. What they want included is an experience along with the meal.

Look around and you will find that most advertisements and commercials center on humor and having a good time. The reason for this is simple. Marketing companies understand that everyone is attracted to entertainment. This is why most (if not all) commercials have humor tied into them. The American consumer is just as interested in being provided with an experience along with the product or service being purchased. In today's world we do not go to a restaurant simply to eat but to be entertained. We want the music along with the canoes and various nostalgia items hanging on the walls and ceilings. Plaster the eating area with sports memorabilia and the restaurant now serves an experience with every food order. We do not go to a clothing store simply to purchase a new outfit. What we are really shopping for is a certain logo to create an image for ourselves.

In terms of dentistry customer service, most organizations need to understand that friendly people will always help to enhance this sense of entertainment that most consumers are after. As an example, theme parks need to hire on the basis of friendliness first. This is because families enter a park with the mindset of having fun. When employees at the park are cheerful and friendly, the overall experience for the customer becomes more meaningful. Fun is definitely what today's consumer is looking for. And when everything is said and done, *it is only the friendly people who are most qualified to enhance this entertaining environment in our experience-driven economy.*

2. Friendly people reach out

*The best place to find a helping hand is at
the end of your own arm.*

Exceptional service is about reaching out and finding what the customer's present needs are. Being friendly helps because customers will be more open about their immediate needs when they sense a friendly person is helping them. On the most part, when someone who does not project kindness is helping a customer, the customer will be less inclined to ask for help. Think of the times that you have entered a business where the service provided was not very friendly. More than likely you were less inclined to ask for assistance. On the other hand, we all have had times of being helped by someone who showed us consideration. In these pleasant experiences we tended to ask more questions about the product or service and then may have purchased the product simply because we were served with kindness.

3. Friendly people are interested in others

Be kind to unkind people – they need it the most.

If you take a good look you will find that friendly people tend to be more others-focused. This is a huge benefit for those in the dentistry customer service industry. Friendly people know a secret. They have learned that being others-focused brings more fulfillment into their lives. Think of it in this way. *If we do not have the attitude of friendliness toward people, we will be less inclined to want to serve them simply because of our lack of interest in meeting their needs.*

This is what I call the "I disease" where life tends to revolve around my needs alone. This of course can be detrimental if our job is to serve others. The reason for this is that great service is always a result of taking our eyes off of ourselves and attending to the needs of others. Showing friendliness accomplishes this.

4. Friendly people earn more trust

Be what you wish others to become.

This is a major factor when it comes to serving our customers. It is a known fact that a friendly attitude will gain a customer's trust more than an unfriendly attitude. Customers will be more inclined to purchase a product or service if we have a friendly personality. This is because we all have a tendency to trust those who are friendlier. In regards to providing excellent dentistry customer service, friendliness must be a top priority in every organization if goals are to be met. If a business fails to understand the importance of showing kindness to their customers, customers will eventually find another company to do business with. *Remember that trust is the bedrock for creating customer loyalty, and the only way to project this is to show kindness to our patrons.*

5. Friendly people see the cup half-full

Being friendly can accomplish much. It causes mistrust, hostility and misunderstanding to disappear.

Another key benefit of having a friendly disposition is that it usually comes as a result of a positive outlook on life. This is important if we are to attract customers. Everyone enjoys being around people who look at life from a positive point of view. This is because deep inside we all would like to see the cup half-full. *(I like to tell people that the cup is overflowing.)*

Because life can have both peaks and valleys, it is always refreshing to come across a person who maintains a consistent attitude throughout both good and trying times. This kind of attitude attracts because we somehow recognize the benefits of seeing life from a more positive viewpoint. Friendly people are the leaders when it comes to maintaining an optimistic outlook on life. They are the ones who become dentistry customer service superstars because of their cheerful mindset. This optimistic personality will not only attract others, but also give us an advantage in providing outstanding service.

6. Friendly people draw others in

*Friendliness is a language the dumb can speak
and the deaf understand.*

As mentioned earlier, people from all walks of life respond positively when others are nice to them. This universal language of kindness is understood everywhere. In the area of dentistry customer service, people will always be attracted when they are served with friendliness. I am always amazed when playing the role of a customer and find myself being served by a person projecting an aloof attitude. My first reaction tends to be one of surprise. I will usually conclude that the inhospitable person is just having an off day and forget about it. *But what would happen if the person projected this unwelcoming personality everyday? More than likely customers would eventually do business elsewhere.* We must remember that friendliness will consistently attract others while unfriendliness will do the opposite and drive customers away faster than any other method.

7. Friendly people have the likable factor

The more friendly and thoughtful a person is, the more friendliness he or she will find in other people.

By now we should understand that dentistry customer service is about finding and meeting the needs of others. One constant need of a customer is to be treated in a kind and respectful manner. A friendly demeanor will also benefit us in that others will tend to rate our service better simply because they appreciate the kindness shown. When we project friendliness, people will also have a tendency to like us more. *Think of those who we tend to like. More than likely they have been kind to us.* Our tendency is to like those who are friendly to us. It is a known fact that likable people have friendly dispositions. This likable factor will not only enhance the overall service experience for every customer, but also give them a reason to do business with us in the future.

8. Friendly people are more involved

*Kindness is the glue by which society
is bound together.*

Another great benefit of cultivating a friendly disposition is that it tends to make us more involved in life. Not only do we attract more friends, but also draw others toward us. Dentistry customer service superstars tend to be more involved simply because of their friendly disposition. When I look back at the friendly people that I have met in the past, I cannot help but see their life being so much more enriched. They have many friends because of their kindheartedness. This benefit also makes us more approachable to those whom we serve. They cannot help but notice our sunny disposition and walk away feeling that our service was excellent.

9. Friendly people are nice to work with

*Speak kindly – it is far better to rule
by love than fear.*

Successful companies are a reflection of an excellent dentistry customer service team. This is essential if a business is going to flourish in providing exceptional service. Teams that succeed are a result of mutual kindness that permeates throughout the company. When employees are friendly toward each other, the overall atmosphere improves. Customers can sense when a dentistry customer service team respects each other because the attitude that the employees project toward each other will soon be reflected in how well the customer is treated. *The winning teams will treat their customers with outstanding service simply as a result of how they treat each other.*

They say that what goes around comes around. This is especially true when management treats their employees in a kind and friendly manner. This will benefit the customer in the end. The saying that happy employees make their customers happy holds true. *A good principle to remember is the golden rule of management that states leaders should treat their employees the way they want their employees to treat their customers.* Being friendly to our co-workers will go a long way in creating an outstanding dentistry customer service team.

10. Friendly people enjoy life more

If you look hard enough you will notice that gracious people tend to enjoy life more. Their friendly demeanor opens up a whole new way of relating to others. A great example is Charles Dicken's fictional character Scrooge in the classic *A Christmas Carol*. The highlight of the novel is when Scrooge has a change of heart and transforms his mean spirit to one of kindness. It becomes clear that his new kindhearted demeanor gives joy to everyone. This instantaneously makes Scrooge much more enjoyable to be around.

In the same way, our friendliness makes our work environment much more pleasant. Not only do we enjoy ourselves more, but others will also take pleasure in being around us. This has huge benefits as dentistry customer service representatives. Our enjoyment on the job will translate into providing better service and creating a more pleasant atmosphere.

11. Friendly people tend to be unselfish

CHAPTER 2

There are three important guidelines for better relationships. The first is to be kind. The second is to be kind. The third is to be kind.

Friendly people tend to be more focused on others and less focused on themselves. This is another key benefit if we are to provide outstanding service. *To be centered on others is a must if great service is to be continually given to our customers.* If we were to again take a close look at people who are consistently friendly, we will find that they tend to be others-centered. This makes it much easier to give excellent service simply because selfishness is a major detriment for delivering great service.

The trait that is found in the majority of dentistry customer service superstars is that they tend to be people who give. They want to help people and have found that the more they focus on others, the less they demand for themselves. *They have found that serving brings about a positive change in their own lives.* This attitude is the key to becoming a service superstar.

12. Friendly people see the best in others

Kindness is loving people more than they deserve.

A final benefit of having the attitude of friendliness is that it tends to help us see the best in others. *The more kindness we show allows us to see our customer's best side. This is because kindness always makes others brighten up.* Being friendly will also make serving easier because of our treatment to others. *People will appreciate that we bring out the best in them.* This will also give customers a reason to speak highly of our service because of the way that we make them feel. Since everyone likes to be at their best, our friendliness toward them will only help to achieve this.

On the other hand, being unfriendly tends to make us look through a different set of lenses. We tend to be more judgmental and see others as interruptions. We eventually become faultfinders in our relationships. We tend to be less welcoming because of our inhospitable manner. Being unfriendly never quite seems to work. Our life becomes more disruptive and people eventually back away from us. This is not good for business and certainly destructive if we are in the job of serving others. In the end, friendliness will always come out on top.

Friendliness starts with a smile

> *"I've never seen a smiling face that was not beautiful."*
> - Unknown

In my first book, *Service Starts with a Smile,* I wrote about sixty-nine reasons why customers return. One of the incentives that draw people back is by making our environment more welcoming. The key is to create a friendly first impression. This can be accomplished simply by offering a pleasant smile to each customer. Without saying a word, this gesture will speak volumes and give a favorable impression to everyone who comes through our door.

> *Don't open a shop unless you like to smile.*
> - Chinese Proverb

The simple smile uses less facial muscles to produce and will create a warm and welcoming atmosphere. Here are five tips to assist in giving away more smiles:

Tip #1   Smiling takes practice

> *Smile - sunshine is good for your teeth.*

In order to become more natural at smiling we need to practice. I know that this sounds odd but somewhere in our growing up years we have forgotten how to smile. Watch an infant and you will notice that most will freely give away smiles. Maybe this is one of the reasons they are so cute. Being able to smile takes a conscious effort for most adults. We somehow have lost this natural ability and would benefit greatly if we simply learned to smile more often. Not only will our looks instantaneously improve, but others will also feel more comfortable around us. *A smile is an inexpensive way to change our looks!* Someone once said that a smile confuses an approaching frown. When we offer a friendly smile, we are in essence showing kindness and creating a welcoming atmosphere for those who we come in contact with. So remember to practice and soon you will notice others smiling back at you.

Tip #2   what are you meditating on?

"Finally, brethren, whatsoever things are true, whatsoever things are honest, whatsoever things are just, whatsoever things are pure, whatsoever things are lovely, whatsoever things are of good report; if there be any virtue, and if there be any praise, think on these things."
                              -Philippians 4:8

I have found that what we meditate on can have a major effect on how much smiling we do on a daily basis. Nothing can evaporate a smile more than keeping our mind on things that bring worry into our life.

> *"Don't tell me that worry doesn't do any good. I know better. The things I worry about never happen."*
> - Unknown

Maybe that is why children can so easily smile. Their minds are not cluttered with a collection of files that remind us to fret. *I believe worrying has to go down as the number one way to waste time.* It has never accomplished anything positive. Maybe it's time to change your thinking if you have lost the natural ability to smile. Starting today begin to think of things that are virtuous. Get into the habit of meditating on right and excellent thoughts. Before long you will find yourself smiling more often. People will soon take notice and return a smile back!

Tip #3   Get rid of the "I Disease"

The measure of friendliness that people show is a reflection of the way we have treated them.

Another sure way to smile less is getting too focused on ourselves. This is what I would call the "I Disease" where life revolves around me, myself and I. Not only is this detrimental to providing great dentistry customer service, but it will also quickly wipe away a friendly smile in no time. *I have found that people who smile easily are unselfish and genuinely show a concern for others.* On the other hand, those who simply live for themselves rarely smile because of the emptiness that selfishness brings. Life is so much more than exclusively trying to meet our own wants and needs. If we truly want to smile more we need to discover that it is only in giving of ourselves that we find joy. Learn to be more interested in helping others and you will soon find yourself smiling more.

Tip #4   Learn to laugh again

A laugh is a smile that bursts.

Laughter truly is like medicine in that it not only will improve our health but also make us learn to smile more. I believe that everyone would benefit if they just took time to laugh. Watch a group of children and we will hear laughter fill the air. Maybe it's the responsibilities of adult life that close the door to spontaneous laughter in later years. Whatever the reason, we need to laugh more.

Some people have described laughter as a great way to take an internal bath. I agree. People who laugh easily are usually the ones who freely give away smiles. *These people also attract others simply because of their carefree nature.* If we want to smile more it may also be worth our efforts to replace any lingering worries with wholesome laughter. Our customers will gladly welcome and appreciate it.

CHAPTER 2

Tip #5   Each day is a gift

Today is a gift; that's why they call it "the present."

Sometimes it can be the elementary reminders that awaken us to the things that really matter. *We need to be reminded that every day of life is truly a gift.* It is important to appreciate this gift if we are to smile more. We have all heard that life is too short to squander away. Every person is allowed 24 hours a day and is given a choice in how they will use it. When we look at life as a moment-by-moment gift that should be enjoyed, we will learn to express this appreciation with a friendlier countenance. This alone should give us all the more reason to smile.

Being friendly toward others is one of the most difficult things to give away - it is usually returned.

♥

The Attitude of

Enthusiasm

Fervent, zeal, eagerness, optimism, excited, inspired, stirred, moved, motivated, wholehearted, passionate.

Chapter 3

The Attitude of Enthusiasm

*Serving with enthusiasm adds to the
customer's overall experience.*

Have you ever met someone who was enthused about something? It could be about anything. More than likely you were drawn in by their zeal. Now imagine coming across someone who was enthused about life. Everything they did was done with interest and excitement. How would that make you feel? More than likely you would be attracted to their passion for living. *The reason for our attraction is that when we are confronted with a person full of enthusiasm, it somehow awakens something inside of us.* We feel something that may have been dormant for years. This is exactly what enthusiasm does to others. It drives them to search into their own lives and wonder whatever happened to the excitement that past dreams and memories once brought.

The attitude of enthusiasm is an invisible force that is felt immediately by others. When we are excited to serve, we will not only excel as dentistry customer service representatives but will have people talking about our great service. Consider the times you have been served exceptionally and you will find that the person did it with enthusiasm. I have personally witnessed dentistry customer service superstars who were so passionate about their product or service that they could not help but serve with enthusiasm. They simply gave their best.

DENTISTRY CUSTOMER SERVICE SUPERSTARS

I am convinced that without enthusiasm dentistry customer service becomes more of a duty to perform. When we are not excited about serving others, we somehow begin to lose our balance in providing our customers with excellent service. On the other hand, when we truly enjoy what we do it will show in the way we perform. No other attitude can make us more passionate about our duties. Being enthused makes others take notice and will consistently deliver better service to our customers. *They walk away and feel that the service was outstanding simply because of our eagerness to serve them.*

Let me share an example of how enthusiasm can decide on the overall experience when serving customers. Recently one evening I took my family for ice cream after church. The ice cream parlor we decided on was more upscale than your typical parlor. In the past we have visited this store and were pleased with the service. When we walked in we were greeted with loud music that would appeal to a very small segment of society (who more than likely would not patronize this place). The two young girls working behind the counter immediately gave the impression by their faces that this was the last place they wanted to be. There would be no friendly greeting or smiles. As we were ready to order our ice cream one of the girls blurted out something to the effect of "please fire me." It was a very odd thing to announce to a customer. They were definitely not thrilled to be there. After leaving I thought of our experience. We were excited to get some ice cream but were immediately turned off by the lack of enthusiasm displayed by the servers. I also thought about how much the owner must be paying for rent at this upscale outdoor mall, and if he realized that these two employees were driving customers away. I believe that someone somewhere had made a severe miscalculation in hiring these two employees. They did not understand basic 101-dentistry customer service.

If I had owned this ice cream parlor, I would hire employees who showed the most enthusiasm. I would want people who were excited to scoop up ice cream. Here is the reason why. Everyone who goes out for ice cream is thrilled about the prospects of tasting their favorite flavor. If this ice cream parlor had simply hired employees who projected the same excitement about serving the ice cream, the whole experience for the customer would be greatly enhanced. Customers would walk away with the feeling that the ice cream is the best around. This not only goes for ice cream parlors, but can also apply to restaurants, theme parks, roller rinks, clothing stores, resorts, insurance companies, and a thousand other organizations. *What we need to understand is that customers on the most part will consider our service dazzling if we simply understand that serving them with enthusiasm would enhance their overall experience.*

Imagine that you and your family decided to go out to your favorite restaurant. When you enter the doors you are greeted in a welcoming manner and seated. A few minutes later a friendly and enthused waitress appears to serve you and your family. All of a sudden the whole experience of going out for dinner is enhanced simply because the people were excited to serve your family. We could easily replace going to a restaurant with getting a haircut. You walk into the store and are greeted kindly with a warm smile and told that it will be five minutes. A few minutes pass and your name is called out by a friendly voice. The hair stylist seems genuinely interested about being able to cut your hair. She then asks about your preferences and you sense that she is really listening as you describe how you would like to look ten years younger. She responds by telling you that she is a beautician not a magician. She then laughs and continues to be enthused about having the honor of cutting your hair. She somehow gives you the impression that you are a VIP customer. After leaving a hefty tip, you walk away feeling that the service was outstanding.

When customers decide to make a purchase on a product or service, they are usually excited about the prospects of acquiring it. *We as dentistry customer service representatives need to realize that our enthusiasm will increase their enthusiasm as well. When we are excited for them, they in turn become more excited about the purchase.* This is important to understand. I am convinced that most bad experiences that customers remember are largely due to being served by a staff that shows no enthusiasm for serving. On the other hand, great experiences are a result of being served by those who are excited about the prospects of serving their customers.

How Can We Be More Enthused?

Having enthusiasm is simply a by-product of having an appreciation for life.

Hopefully we have made the point that enthusiasm can greatly enhance the overall experience for the customer. But how do we become more enthused about the prospects of serving others? What will inspire and motivate us to see serving as a privilege? If having enthusiasm has so many positive benefits, then why doesn't everyone develop more excitement into their lives? These are great questions. *My first thought is that enthusiasm must come from a sincere appreciation for life. When we see life as a gift not to be wasted, our whole outlook will be positively changed.* We will begin to see that each day is to be lived with passion and zeal. This new appreciation that life is a gift will not only enhance our daily lives but also carry over in serving others with enjoyment and passion.

I have always been fascinated by the true stories of those who were in dire straits and somehow survived a life and death situation. I have read accounts of those who survived after floating on a raft in the middle of the ocean for over thirty days with no food. Other true stories that have continually grabbed my attention describe men and women who survived being lost or trapped in uninhabited locations for days on end with little hope of survival. I have also read accounts of those who survived prisoner of war camps and somehow made it through to find freedom once again. Without exception, every one of these brave people who survived such grim circumstances had one commonality: *They all appreciated the simple gift of life after being rescued. We find that these people developed a new enthusiasm and appreciation for simply being alive.*

Maybe you know of someone who has survived a near fatal auto accident or a sickness that had threatened their life. Maybe that someone was you. Whatever the case may be, *people in these situations tend to come out with a deeper appreciation for life.* I believe this occurs because getting through a life-threatening experience makes these survivors appreciate that they are given a

Chapter 3

second chance at life. These survivors wake up each morning and recognize that life is precious and not to be taken for granted. *They have a new belief that every day is a gift.*

I bring up these moving survivor stories to say that we can live with enthusiasm if we see life as a gift. I would like to think that every person has the ability to recapture this enthusiasm for life without having to survive on a raft for thirty days in the middle of a shark-infested ocean. *Having enthusiasm is simply a by-product of having an appreciation for life.* We do not need to go through dire straits to appreciate that life is to be lived with enjoyment. Those who are grateful for the gift of life show it by their passion. I believe that this is the key if we are to serve others with more enthusiasm.

There is a song that I have heard on the radio that captures the essence of seeing life as a gift. These lyrics describe perfectly how we should treasure life:

There is a man who waits for the tests
To see if the cancer has spread yet
And now he asks, "So why did I wait to live till it was time to die?"
If I could have the time back how I'd live
Life is such a gift
So how does the story end?
Well this is your story and it all depends
So don't let it become true
Get out and do what we are meant to do

We live we love
We forgive and never give up
Cause the days we are given are gifts from above
Today we remember to live and to love
We live we love
We forgive and never give up
Cause the days we are given are gifts from above
Today we remember to live and to love

Superchick - We Live© 2005

Ten Benefits of Enthusiasm

*None are as old as those who have
outlived enthusiasm.*

Being an enthusiastic person on and off the job adds so much more to our lives. As mentioned earlier, *enthusiasm attracts simply because it awakens something in others.* This attitude allures others because they see how much we enjoy life. Enthusiastic people have an appreciation for life that draws others in. Being enthused to serve will only add to the overall experience for the customer. They in turn appreciate the fact that we have served them with enjoyment. Customers will give our service a higher rating because of this attitude. They in turn will walk away with a bit of enthusiasm themselves simply because of our zest for serving them. Let's look at ten additional benefits that an attitude of enthusiasm will bring into our lives.

1. Enthusiastic people are excited about getting up in the morning

*Enthusiasm glows, radiates and immediately
captures everyone's attention.*

Think of the most enthused person that you know and you will find that he or she is excited about the simple things in life. There seems to be an inner appreciation that is connected to this attitude. As mentioned earlier, the benefit of serving with enthusiasm will enhance the overall experience for our customers.

*I never did a day's work in my life.
It was all fun.*
- Thomas A. Edison

CHAPTER 3

Enthusiasm will also help us improve serving others because our excitement for life will carry over in how we take care of our customers. Over the years I have come to the conclusion that those who serve best have all had a hint of excitement and gave the impression that they were honored to help. My most memorable experiences as a customer have been moments of being served by people who clearly displayed an enjoyment in what they were doing. They gave the impression that they were excited. *Their contagious enthusiasm also made me more enthused about the product or service being purchased.*

2. Enthusiastic people turn no's into yes's

Just say no to negativism.
- Bumper Sticker

This benefit is huge when it comes to dentistry customer service. Enthusiastic people tend to say yes much more than they say no. *When we are excited about serving others, we will have a tendency to say yes more to our customers.* On the other hand, I have seen unenthused dentistry customer service representatives who acted as though they were excited to say no to their customers. Being a person who can turn no's into yes's will not only draw customers back but make the overall experience more enjoyable. Enthusiastic people tend to give better service and will find any way possible to meet whatever need there is. This attitude makes the service provided a more positive experience because of the optimistic outlook that enthusiasm communicates to others.

3. Enthusiastic people treasure time

*As long as enthusiasm holds out, so will
new opportunities.*

When we are enthused about something in life, time seems to slip away faster. Just the opposite occurs whenever we tend to be bored.

Time then seems to take forever. Enthusiasm has a way of making the clock move quickly simply because we are in an exciting frame of mind. *This is why boredom is so detrimental to our performance on the job. Whenever monotony settles in, we become less motivated.* Our service to others eventually slips because of our lack of enjoyment. That is why having an enthusiastic outlook on the job will help us to perform at a much higher level. Not only will our workday tend to go faster, but also our performance at serving others will drastically improve. It is our enthusiasm that makes time fly.

I am convinced that one of the most damaging attitudes that can weaken our ability to serve well is allowing boredom to enter our lives. *We will soon find ourselves less motivated to serve and more likely to lose interest in our job. This is why it is so important to enjoy our occupation.* When we take pleasure in our vocation, we will not only work more productively, but also wonder where the time went.

4. Enthusiastic people tend to be happier

Success on the job can be measured by the amount of enthusiasm we had in our career.

I truly believe that happy employees make happy customers. When we are happy on the job, our customers will take notice by the excellent service that we provide for them. This is why having an attitude of enthusiasm is so important on the job. *Think of the times that you have felt happy in life. More than likely being enthusiastic about something caused it.* Maybe we captured our enthusiasm simply in recognition that life itself is a gift to be treasured. Whatever the reason, one of the triggers that made us happy was having an attitude of enthusiasm. They really do go hand-in-hand. We will always perform at our best when we enjoy our profession. Being enthused about serving is no different. When we enjoy our work we will show it by our enthusiasm and satisfaction. These two traits will be recognized by the excellent service we provide to our customers.

CHAPTER 3

5. Enthusiastic people use their gifts

When enthusiasm is taken to the job, the job will become more alive with exciting new possibilities.

Every person has certain gifts and talents that they are naturally born with. *One way of finding out whether or not we are using these gifts in our occupation is to simply ask if we are enthused on the job.* This of course is not to imply that everyday will be filled with anticipated excitement as we leave for work. What it does mean is that on the most part we enjoy our occupation. This alone can be a sign of whether or not we are using our gifts. It is a pretty good sign that a person may be utilizing his or her gifts if they tend to enjoy themselves on the job. *On the other hand, when a person shows a lack of enthusiasm on the job, he or she may be in a wrong position.*

When I am a customer and am being served by someone who displays a total lack of enthusiasm, I somehow sense that they are not in the right position to use their true gifts. This can have a negative effect on customers who can sense that the person waiting on them would rather be somewhere else. This is why it is so important to hire employees who are excited about the prospects of serving others. This is a sign that they will also be great as dentistry customer service representatives. *Creating an excellent dentistry customer service team can be defined as having a group of people who are using their natural talents and gifts. Their enthusiasm becomes a by-product of being able to use their true talents.*

6. Enthusiastic people see solutions

Any great movement in the pages of history has been the result of enthusiasm.

Another great benefit of having an attitude of enthusiasm is that it tends to help us see solutions more clearly. This inner attitude allows us to focus more on finding solutions and less on clinging to problems.

Enthusiasm gives us the motivation needed to seek answers. We become better at problem solving. Setbacks are looked at as challenges. This will only make us better at serving our customers because of various roadblocks that can arise during a course of a day. Our focus on seeking solutions also gives us a more positive outlook in life. We stop dwelling on problems and begin seeking solutions. This has a big impact on how well we deliver service to our customers. They will sense that we are doing our best to serve them because of our positive outlook at meeting their needs.

7. Enthusiastic people are interested in learning

Some have enthusiasm for 30 minutes, some for 30 days, but it is the man who has it for 30 years who makes a success of his life.

When we are enthusiastic we tend to want to continue learning. This of course is a very good trait to have both on and off the job. It is a known fact that when we are interested in learning a particular subject, our ability to comprehend increases tremendously. I have found that the learning curve will always increase when people are enthusiastic about wanting to learn. This has tremendous value for those in the workplace. The best employees tend to be those who have a desire to improve by becoming more educated. This also goes for those who serve customers. Not only will they excel in meeting the needs of their customers, but also will continue to seek better ways of doing their jobs. This enthusiasm will benefit their job performance simply because they want to improve on their skills.

8. Enthusiastic people show appreciation

Enthusiasm allows us to appreciate life more.

The eighth benefit that enthusiastic people have is how easily they can convey to the customer their appreciation. Customers will always be thankful when we show how much we appreciate their business. There is something to be said about giving others the sense that they

CHAPTER 3

are appreciated. *If we as dentistry customer service representatives could grasp how powerful expressing gratitude is to our customers, we would take every opportunity to show more appreciation.* I am convinced that letting our customers know how much we value them will bring them back time and again. I also believe that the people who are most qualified to express appreciation to others are those who have an attitude of enthusiasm. Think of the times that someone showed you appreciation. More than likely you remembered it simply because of their excitement and sincere gratitude. As dentistry customer service representatives, our customers will remember our sincere appreciation if we express it with sincere enthusiasm. *Without this, the expression of gratitude tends to lack authenticity.*

9. Enthusiastic people send a message

Genius is nothing more than inflamed enthusiasm.

When we are enthused about the product or service we are selling, our attitude will send a message to the customer. This is important because of the feeling of self-assurance that it will give to those who are served by us. *The message that we express with our enthusiastic attitude conveys that we are confident that the product or service will meet the customer's immediate needs.* As an example, if we were in the restaurant business and hired servers who believed that the food tasted excellent, we would want to make sure that they positively expressed this to every patron who entered our doors. The best way to do this would be to have employees who knew how to communicate enthusiasm when being asked about a certain item on the menu. If we express with excitement that the chicken potpie is the best in town *(and we truly believe it),* our way of expressing this to our patrons would assure them that it would be a great choice. This is why it is so important to hire people who are enthused about the product or service that we are presenting to the customer. This attitude alone sends a secure feeling to our customers and will give them the self-assurance that they have made the right choice.

10. Enthusiastic people make things happen

Some of the world's greatest feats were accomplished by people not smart enough to know they were impossible.

The final benefit in having an enthusiastic attitude is that it allows us to make things happen. By this I mean that enthusiasm has a way of motivating us to get things done in an efficient manner. Because of our positive outlook, we are better equipped to meet the customer's immediate needs in a timely fashion. *Without enthusiasm, we would be less motivated and willing to give our customers the best service possible.* Having this attitude jumpstarts our motivation to take care of others. On the other hand, being unmotivated is essentially a sign that a person lacks enthusiasm. This deficiency can be detrimental if our job is to serve others. Being enthused will give us a big advantage in that it will inspire us to deliver outstanding service. *I have found that every dentistry customer service superstar that I have encountered can make things happen simply because they were motivated to make my experience as pleasurable as possible.* This never would have been the case if they had lacked the enthusiasm to serve. In the final analysis, people with enthusiasm will always be the best qualified to make things happen in order to provide the best possible service to their customers.

Success is going from failure to failure without a loss of enthusiasm.
- Winston Churchill

♥

The Attitude of

Caring

Understanding, thoughtful, selfless, attentive, compassionate, gentle, concerned, loving, and considerate.

Chapter 4

The Attitude of Caring

Loyalty occurs when customers sense that we genuinely care.

Of all attitudes in existence, none is more powerful than the attitude of caring about others. This attitude alone will determine the outcome of every relationship in life. It far outweighs any other attitude simply because it is the cornerstone by which every other attitude will manifest itself. No other attitude will determine our fate quite like how much we care for others. In essence, caring will be the attitude that will ultimately measure the qualities of our relationships both on and off the job. When we truly have a heart that cares for others, our life will begin to take on more meaning. Customers will also quickly take notice of our sincere desire to serve them when we care about their needs. Loyalty also begins to happen when our customers sense that meeting their needs is more important than simply making a sale.

We feel reassured when we sense that another person cares about us. It provides for us a feeling of security and support. It also reinforces our connection with others. *Caring is one of the best things we can do for our health.*

As mentioned earlier, this attitude will have a major influence on every other attitude that has taken a hold of us. When we care about others, we will find that our disposition will be friendlier. We will be more respectful and tend to encourage others more frequently. Customers will also be more attracted to us because they will sense that we truly care about them. Without having to say anything, they will quickly sense by our actions that we can be trusted and will do whatever it takes to meet their immediate needs. On the other hand, customers will sense when we do not care about meeting their needs. Whether we care or not will be projected in various ways to them. This attitude is difficult to hide because of the many signs that eventually come out. Let's look at a few ways that customers will sense whether or not we truly care.

The face cannot hide

The first sign that customers will always measure when they are about to be served is a quick read of the face. Whether we realize it or not, every one of us eventually becomes proficient at reading others simply by doing an inventory of their facial expressions. A quick glance can indicate whether or not the person is interested in meeting our needs. One of the first areas that we look at is the person's eyes. They say that the eyes are the windows to the soul. Studying a person's eyes can tell us a lot about whether or not the person is interested in helping us or simply performing a duty. As dentistry customer service representatives, it's important to let both our eyes and smiles come through loud and clear. *Friendly eyes matched with a friendly smile will not only tell our customers that we are happy to see them, but will also convey that we genuinely care.* That is one major reason that a friendly smile can go a long way in expressing that we care.

The tone of our voice

Don't look at me in that tone of voice!

It's been said that the tone of our voice accounts for approximately 38% of what the listener gets from the message, 55% from our body language, and only 7% from what is actually being said. *As humans, we quickly adapt our listening more to the tone of what is being said and less on what actually is said.* Our customers will measure us in the same manner. It is important to allow our tone of voice to speak in such a way as to convey to our customers that we care about meeting their needs. One simple way to do this is by learning to talk to our customers and not at them. A friendly tone of voice will express that we care. Learning to speak clearly and in a gracious manner will give others the impression that we are there for them.

Actions speak louder than words

> *He that does good to another does*
> *good also to himself.*
> -Seneca

We have all heard the expression that actions speak louder than words. When everything is said and done, the measurement of whether or not we care about our customers will always be revealed by our actions. Words are just words until we put some shoe leather to them. As mentioned in earlier chapters, our first priority as service representatives is to take care of our customer's immediate needs. The way to do this to make sure our words match our actions. If we make a promise it is paramount that we follow-up with an action to that promise. When we show this through consistent follow-up action, our customers will eventually develop loyalty because of the trust that we have earned from them. Our actions express to them that we truly do care.

Developing an Attitude of Caring

Caring about others provides us with the key for unlocking better relationships and making them more genuine.

Because caring has a major influence on every other attitude that we carry with us, it is important that we take an inventory of how much care we project to our customers. *I am convinced that every other attitude will be changed for the better when we learn to care more about others, including our customers.* In order to develop a more caring attitude, the first step that must occur is to take a personal inventory of how much we truly care. I know this seems like an odd thing to ask, but how can we improve in this area unless we take an honest look and measure if there is any room for improvement. Do we project to our customers *(and others for that matter)* that we genuinely want to meet their needs, or do they sense that we are just doing what the job demands? There is a big difference in these two attitudes, and both will be reflected in how well we serve. Customers will be able to tell in no time how much care we put into our service.

Once we have taken a closer, more personal look at our own measure of caring, we then will want to consider ways to improve on developing genuine concern for the needs of others. As mentioned, I am convinced that this attitude alone would begin to transform any organization. Customers will sense this and begin to tell others about their wonderful experience. If we are to look at improving this attitude, it may help to discover what caring actually looks like in real life. *I have found four traits that have been evident in every person that I have found who consistently portrays a caring attitude.* Let's look at these four characteristics and see if they can help us to discover how we can become better at caring for others.

Four Traits commonly found in a caring attitude

#1 Patience reflects a caring attitude

> *"How far you go in life depends on your being tender with the young, compassionate with the aged, sympathetic with the striving and tolerant of the weak and strong. Because someday in life you will have been all of these."*
> - George Washington Carver

One of the first traits that I have consistently found in people with a caring attitude is their ability to be patient. Not only will this attract others, but will also become a major advantage for those who display patience when serving others. As dentistry customer service representatives, having patience will always make our customers feel more comfortable. The reason for this is because when we display a

Chapter 4

sense of serenity for every type of situation that is bound to occur, our customers are given comfort in knowing we will be able to meet their needs in a professional and efficient manner. This is due to the fact that patient people tend to be more calm in various situations.

The more we care for the welfare of others, the more we will begin to notice how others care for us. We begin to find that what goes around eventually comes around.

Being a patient person is a virtue that is esteemed throughout the world. Every society considers this trait to be highly valued. *The reason for this is that it conveys a sense of self-control in the one who consistently shows to be patient with others.* Whenever I sense that I am being served by a patient person, my sense of importance is suddenly enhanced. I feel that this person is giving me the right to express my immediate needs as a customer without feeling that I am intruding on his or her time. *Patient people also have a way of making us feel accepted simply by their calm disposition. This of course creates an atmosphere that is warm and welcoming.*

Being patient with others may come easy to those who tend to have the genetic make-up of being more understanding. But this does not mean that we cannot all learn to be a little more patient with others. I have discovered that times of testing our character are great proving grounds for developing more patience. Whenever we may go through a difficult situation in our own lives, it can become the perfect climate for exercising more patience. I have found that those who tend to be more patient with people have personally experienced difficulties in the past that eventually made them more understanding toward others. I believe these times of trials can also help to develop more character if we will only learn from them.

Patience is the companion of wisdom.
- St. Augustine

#2   Listening reflects a caring attitude

Much silence makes a powerful noise.

When I first met my wife Carol at college, I was immediately impressed with her ability to listen. As I babbled away I could not help but notice how she continued to pay attention to what I had to say. Over the years I have watched how my wife has attentively listened to other people. She truly is gifted with the "art of listening." *When we listen to others we are conveying to them that we care about what they have to say. We also are acknowledging their worth simply because we are giving them our undivided attention and allowing them to speak with no interruptions.* This alone can have a powerful effect on others because it allows them to convey what they are thinking and gives the person a sense of importance. Another great benefit of listening is that it will always express consideration for others. To listen intently truly is one of the finest gifts that we can give to another person.

Listening is an attitude of the heart, a genuine desire to be with another that both attracts and heals.

Now imagine how our customers feel when we intently listen to what they have to say. When we give our full attention it conveys to them that we care about their needs. This automatically gives our customers a sense that we are there for them and want their experience to be as enjoyable as possible. Customers will also rate our service more positive simply because we have taken the time to listen to what they have to say. They will walk away feeling validated and understood because of the consideration that we have communicated to them through the simple act of listening.

A good listener is not only popular everywhere, but after a while he knows something.

Chapter 4

I am convinced that this gift can transform and help to develop healthier relationships. People will begin to be more honest with us because they will sense that we care about them. *Very rarely have I met someone who gave me the impression that they cared who did not listen well. It is as if caring and listening consistently go hand-in-hand.* I have always thought that if someone put an advertisement in the paper that simply stated they would do nothing but listen for a full hour, people would flock to them for the opportunity to express their thoughts without being interrupted.

It is the province of knowledge to speak and the privilege of wisdom to listen.

When we serve customers, it gives us the perfect opportunity to listen more and speak less. This is because we are there to meet their needs. But if we do not listen, it will be difficult to understand what their needs are. Listening allows us to give our customers the sense that we really care enough to want to give them what they would like, and not what we think they should have. We are showing them by our attentiveness that we care about them. This alone creates a wonderful experience for those we serve. Our listening allows them an opportunity to express their needs.

Asking questions shows our desire to listen

One of the greatest compliments we can give to a person is to ask their opinion and then listen closely to what they have to say.

When we do not listen to our customers we convey that we are not interested in meeting their needs. This can be detrimental to any business. Let's use an example. If I sold a certain product I would ask questions and find out exactly what the customer is looking for. *This would tell them right away that I am more interested in what they want and less on what I would like to sell them.* Being able to ask questions is a wonderful way to show others that we are listeners. Being able to ask the right questions is a gift that allows customers to open up. If we are to consistently deliver outstanding service, our goal must be to meet and exceed our customer's expectations. The only way we will be able to do this is to make inquires that will then allow the customer to openly share. This also will give the feeling that we are there for them.

"The greatest gift we can give another is our undivided attention.

The interest that is conveyed by our questions will then give each customer a positive reason to speak highly of our service. It is the combination of asking the right questions and listening intently that will win our customers.

#3   Acceptance reflects a caring attitude

When people are asked to remember a person who meant a lot to them in life, they usually remember someone who really cared and understood them.

Another telling sign of a caring attitude is being able to accept others unconditionally. Having this characteristic in our personality is powerful in attracting customers. The reason for this is that we all appreciate when others show us acceptance. It is as if we have an inner need to be received by others. When we have a caring attitude, others will soon take notice of the way we show acceptance toward them. This is essential if we are to attract customers because of the wide range of people that we will be serving on a daily basis. When we express to others a sense of acceptance, they in turn feel more comfortable and will want to come back in the future.

One of the most important goals of any organization is to create an environment for the customer that is friendly and welcoming. This can only occur when we communicate unconditional acceptance toward those who walk through our doors. Consistently giving this sense of welcoming to customers will have a positive influence on their decision to return. Over the years I have had experiences as a customer that has made me realize the importance of feeling accepted. There have been memories with a variety of organizations that have been both pleasant and not so pleasant. *As I recall these experiences, I am always amazed to see how the level of acceptance I felt determined my overall rating for the service that was provided.* The companies that I felt provided excellent service had a way of making their customers feel welcomed and accepted.

Providing our customers a sense of acceptance will go a long way in making them feel more welcomed at our establishment. In the mind of the customer, if the service starts off with a friendly welcome, they will give our service a higher rating. *This is why it will make all the difference if we simply give each customer a warm and friendly welcome.* This alone is the key in providing them with a sense of acceptance. Not only will we show that we care but also give them a reason to want to return.

#4   Being nice reflects a caring attitude

*Genuine kindness is doing something nice
for someone who will never find out.*

A final characteristic of a caring attitude is that it will show itself through kindheartedness. Caring people tend to always be kind and friendly toward others. *I have never met someone who I considered to be caring who did not also show kindness toward others.* This caring attitude has consistently showed itself through benevolence. Reflect on the times of meeting someone who you considered to be friendly. More than likely you enjoyed their presence because of the way they made you feel. *If we look deeper, we will find that they were liked because of a kind attitude toward us. This caring is what true relationships are built upon.*

In chapter one I focused on the attitude of friendliness and how influential it is in providing outstanding dentistry customer service. The reason for this is because when we show ourselves to be friendly toward others, we are sending them a message of acceptance. *We are also meeting a basic need of giving them a sense of belonging. Kindness has a way of doing this.* Without kindness, our customers will sense that they are not welcomed and will look for the nearest exit door.

Customers who may consider doing business are measuring us by how accepted we make them feel. The intelligent managers understand this and focus on creating a friendly atmosphere by hiring those who have what I had earlier coined *the friendly factor*. These are people who tend to have a disposition that consistently shows consideration toward others. When companies understand this and hire friendly people to meet and greet the customer, there will be a sudden change in how each customer perceives the service provided. *Customers who encounter these organizations that hire based on the friendly factor will desire to come back simply because of the acceptance felt every time they enter the doors.*

On the other hand, when a company does not take into account the power of friendliness, they can miss out in hiring the right people for the job. I have often thought that hiring people who will be working with the public should first and foremost be based on being able to communicate in a kind and friendly manner. Of course this can be difficult because of the problem of how to measure kindness. But if the hiring team can learn to ask the right questions, they may be able to hire the candidates who have the friendly factor. *Hiring the right people can make or break the customer's perception of the service provided.*

The power of caring

Men are only as great as they are kind.

I hope by now we recognize how influential a caring attitude is on every organization that provides dentistry customer service. As mentioned earlier, caring about others is the foundation by which every other attitude grows out from. When we care about others our life will reflect such character traits as being kind to others, showing respect, and appreciating what people do for us. Let's look at a list of esteemed qualities that will shine forth when we genuinely have a caring heart.

We will be patient toward others

As discussed earlier, patience is one of the qualities that a caring attitude will consistently bring forth. Not only will our customers quickly take notice when we serve them with a heart of patience, but they will be more receptive toward us.

We will listen more

The first duty of caring is to listen.

As mentioned earlier, the more we listen, the more it will show that we care. When we give the gift of listening to our customers, they in turn will consistently give our service a higher rating. Listening does two important things for our customers. First it conveys our concern about meeting their needs. Second, and more importantly, it validates that we care.

We will be less selfish

No man is more cheated than the selfish man.

Another valued characteristic that a caring attitude will bring forth is selflessness. This is because caring makes us focus more on others and less on ourselves. This is one of the beautiful features of capturing an attitude that cares for others. Whether we realize it or not, customers will notice when we are more focused on ourselves because of the attitude that selfishness tends to bring forth. This "all about me" attitude also makes it difficult to provide exceptional service simply because of an unwillingness to take our eyes off of ourselves. But when we begin to focus on others and their needs, our entire life begins to become more fulfilling.

We will be more understanding

*The capacity to care is the thing which gives
our life its deepest significance.*

When we have an attitude of caring it will also make us more understanding toward others. *We will begin to be more thoughtful with our words and actions.* Understanding simply means that we begin to sense what others may be feeling. As dentistry customer service representatives, having this sensitivity will help us to understand how customers would like to be treated. We will begin to recognize actions in our own conduct that may be detrimental in being able to deliver excellent service. *We also will begin to ask ourselves if we are treating others the way that we would like to be treated.* By learning to be more understanding, our attitude will begin to change and make a big difference in how we deliver service toward others.

We will show more concern

In about the same degree as you are helpful, you will be happy.

An attitude of caring will show itself in our concern for others. People will sense that we are concerned about their welfare because of the way we treat them. When we show concern, it allows our customers to trust us and feel more comfortable in our presence. But if our actions do not reflect that we care, our customers will be less likely to trust our product or service. As a result, our organization will suffer because customers will eventually find a place where they feel others can be trusted by the genuine concern that is shown.

We will be more confident

Chapter 4

People who think about others will also be more confident simply because a caring heart reflects inner security. *The act of caring about others takes a measure of security. When we are weighted down with inner insecurities, it becomes much harder to genuinely care.* The reason for this is that when we are insecure, it becomes more difficult to open up to meet the needs of others. Having a caring attitude can be said to be a reflection of inner confidence.

We will have more empathy

> *Being empathic is the basis of morality.*

Being empathic toward others is a sign that we have an attitude of caring. *Empathetic people have the ability to step inside another person and feel what they may be experiencing at any given moment.* One of the main reasons that this attitude is considered a virtue is because it allows us to be more accepting and less judgmental toward others. We learn to give people the benefit of the doubt and in turn become more considerate for what others may be going through.

We will be more sharing

People who genuinely care for others show it by their willingness to share. By this I mean that they are more willing to give of themselves more often. Like selflessness, having the gift of sharing allows us to focus our attention on meeting the needs of others. We become more others-focused and less me-focused. The saying that states "sharing is caring" holds true. In the end, it is only when we have a heart of caring that will allow us to gladly share and serve others with no reservations.

We will be more sincere

> *Customers will be able to tell the difference between required courtesy and sincere care.*

The final quality that a caring attitude will project to others is a sincerity to serve them. I find this to be one of the most important qualities that caring people have in common. *To be sincere in our caring simply means that there are no strings attached. Our reasons for caring are not tainted with hidden agendas. We care with no ulterior motive.* Our heart is right because we genuinely care for the welfare of others. Customers cannot help but be attracted to this type of service because they will sense our sincere concern for them. Offering outstanding dentistry customer service can be summed up in the following thought:

In the final analysis, providing outstanding dentistry customer service will only work when we genuinely care about our customers.

♥

The Attitude of

Respect

Admiration, high opinion, deference, esteem, reverence, value, regard, good opinion, honor, venerate.

Chapter 5

The Attitude of Respect

*Giving respect shows our willingness
to serve others.*

There is one attitude that every person longs to receive from others. It does not matter if the person is eight or eighty. It makes no difference whether the person resides in a remote village in the middle of nowhere or makes his or her home in a major city. Each one of us is openly receptive when others express it to us. This attractive attitude that I am talking about is when we show others respect. There is no attitude quite as appealing as when we genuinely communicate our respect. It not only validates others, but also gives them a sense of dignity. *When we encounter a person who is respectful toward us, we tend to straighten up and present our best selves to them. This is the beauty and benefit of showing respect. It allows us to bring out the best in people.*

When we have self-respect, it becomes easy to give respect to others. I have found that there is no greater attitude for being our best both on and off the job than having self-respect. It is something that allows us to be all that we can be. As service representatives, when we show our customers respect, we are conveying to them that we have self-respect as well as a willingness to serve them. *This attitude also gives our customers a sense of honor and admiration because of the high regard that is communicated through respect.* It gives our customers a feeling that we admire and appreciate that they have decided to do business with us. This feeling should consistently be conveyed. Customers are important and without them our organization would eventually close.

The mentality that every service representative should have is one where he or she views the customer as essential to the overall success of the business. When we look at customers as the ones who will help to make our business successful, our attitude toward them will begin to change in a more positive manner. The key in winning loyalty starts with respect.

Do we just give respect to anyone?

Treat everyone with kindness, even those who may be rude to you – not because they are nice, but because you are.

Some will say that respect is something that must be earned. It's been said that unless a person has earned respect, we do not have to grant it to him or her. But is this really the way that it should be? Are we to show respect only to those who deserve it? We have all known people who tended to be deficient in the area of self-respect. They not only show little respect for themselves, but also rarely show it to others. Is it then all right to withhold showing respect to those who appear to be without self-respect? What about those people *(including our customers)* who rarely show respect to us? Does this give us an excuse to treat them the way that they have treated us? These are tough questions, but let me share a thought that may help.

Let's say that we lived in a perfect world where everyone treated each other with dignity and respect. If this were the case, it would be easy to treat each person with the same kind of respect that we continually received. But of course this is not the case. We live in a world where every person can fall into a moment of not showing someone proper courtesy. This especially can be the case when our job is to serve customers. We never know what is coming next. The day may be going great when out of the clear blue we encounter a customer who may be having an off day. So what happens? Out of nowhere we have just been spoken to in an ill-mannered tone of voice. Caught by surprise, we take a deep breath in an attempt to compose ourselves for what may be ahead. Without warning, we have just encountered a

Chapter 5

customer who may be looking for someone to take some frustration out on. Do we give it right back or is there a better way to handle this disrespect that was just shown to us?

> *We should be too big to take offense*
> *and too noble to give it.*
> — Abraham Lincoln

There is a better way

The way to find out if we truly have a servant's heart is examine our attitude when others actually treat us like a servant.

As long as we work with customers, we will encounter those who may be having a difficult day. For all we know, they may have just received a parking ticket or lost a dear friend. Whatever the case may be, there is a better way to handle disrespectful behavior toward us. And what is that way? *Show them respect!* I know what you may be thinking right now. In your mind you are saying that it is much easier to say than to do. *But giving our discontented customer a dose of respect will 99.9% of the time make them embarrassed that they have just treated us in such an ill-mannered way.* It's important to understand that our goal is not to embarrass anyone or try to seek revenge in any way. *Our goal if we are to become dentistry customer service superstars is simply to help them out in the best possible way. Showing respect after being disrespected is the best way to handle impolite manners.* The reason for this is that it not only will calm the majority of customers, but will also help the customer to realize that their behavior was inappropriate. *We did not have to say a word.* Our actions in maintaining our own self-respect will show our unhappy customer that we also care about them even though they may have treated us in a disrespectful manner. In the end, it may even come about that our unhappy customer apologizes for their behavior and becomes our most valued customer in the future!

How do we become more respectful?

Self-respect permeates all aspects of our life.

If respecting others is one of the highest virtues in human relationships, why is it so difficult for some to do? *I believe one main reason is because of a lack of self-respect. If we do not have respect for ourselves, how can we expect to give it to others?* In other words, how can we value another person if we do not value ourselves?

How can we give respect to others if we have little respect for ourselves?

When we respect ourselves it becomes much easier to express a healthy admiration toward others. Having self-dignity is the best platform for living with an attitude of respect. I believe the true superstars of dentistry customer service have this as their advantage. Not only do they maintain their own self-respect, but they also have no difficulty in showing others good old-fashioned courtesy.

Integrity unlocks the door to self-respect

Honor is better than honors.
- Abraham Lincoln

One of the best ways to live with an attitude of respect toward both self and others is to maintain integrity in our own lives. As I have pondered on this word through the years, I cannot help but see that *it is only in living with inner integrity that will allow us to project an authentic attitude of respect toward others.* When we have such virtues as honesty, truthfulness, and sincerity, our life will begin to be marked with integrity. *When we live with these honorable qualities, being respectful toward customers is then not determined by their attitude, but by our inner convictions to treat each person with dignity.* We do not allow others to decide how we will treat them. When we have inner integrity, our ego will not be so fragile that we must protect it every time we are hurt or offended. *Our decision to treat others*

Chapter 5

respectfully is based on our inner integrity and not on their behavior toward us. In other words, our personal convictions to treat each person with consideration and respect will not be based on how well they have treated us.

Integrity is such a strong word. When spoken it has a way of making us stand taller and of showing our best side. This virtue can never be bought or given by another person. Integrity can only be maintained on the inside of each individual. If we are to be our best at serving others, it is paramount that we periodically examine ourselves. Let's take a look and learn what integrity is all about.

Nine benefits of integrity

*Respect cannot be purchased or acquired
- it can only be earned from within.*

1. What is inside matches what is outside

In order to maintain a high level of integrity, we need to examine ourselves from time to time and make sure that what is being displayed on the outside is the equivalent of what is on the inside. When we walk with dignity, our job and life will function much smoother. Providing excellent dentistry customer service will begin to happen automatically because of the way we conduct ourselves. *We will be more real in showing respect because it will naturally flow from within. We will not have any personal conflicts because our inner self will be a duplicate of who we claim to be on the outside.*

2. No need to hide anything

The measure of a man's real character is what he would do if he knew he never would be found out.

When we walk with integrity, we become free from having to camouflage anything that may be in conflict with who we represent ourselves to be in front of others. Having integrity allows us to be ourselves because we actually match who we truly are to the outside world. Our life becomes comparable to an open book where the pages are accessible for anyone to read. In terms of providing outstanding service, we will consistently do our best because of the outward qualities that flow from an internal life of integrity.

3. Being temperate in all things

> *No man is fit to command another that cannot command himself.*
> - William Penn

Integrity has a way of making us temperate in all things. We begin to develop a more balanced life both on and off the job. If we are to show others respect on a consistent basis, it is important that we live a life that is self-controlled and moderate in all things. Being able to maintain personal integrity eventually brings us more satisfaction because of the self-control that we have developed. Our job of serving others will also be one of enjoyment simply because of our well-balanced lifestyle.

4. Integrity helps us to endure

Because life can be filled with various surprises along the way, maintaining integrity will help us endure the trials that may come. Integrity has a way of giving us the confidence that we may need to bear whatever may come. *This life of living with self-respect allows us to reach in and find extra strength to handle whatever may come our way.* Because we do not have anything to hide, we are then allowed to build an inner reserve that will get us through any difficulty. In serving others, we will be able to give our best because we now have much to give. The setbacks are only temporary. This strength can only come when we walk with integrity.

CHAPTER 5

5. The greatest leaders have integrity

*Respect yourself and you will soon find
others doing the same.*

Integrity is a key component in leadership and will ultimately determine the willingness of people to follow that leadership. When leaders uphold high standards in their personal lives, people will not only trust their decision-making but will also want to follow them. *There is major difference in wanting to follow a person's leadership versus having to follow due to the position that the leader may hold.* The best leaders are those who are trustworthy and genuinely care about the people who they may lead. With integrity and self-respect, this will naturally occur.

In the best examples of excellent management, people will always choose a leader who can be trusted and lives a lifestyle that reflects honesty, dignity, and self-respect. *This is why people with solid moral principles will always make the best leaders. They can be trusted, and this alone will bring out the best in those they lead.* Without such virtues as honesty, sincerity, and self-respect, leadership will always be flawed because of the lack of trust. Serving others is no different. Customers who sense that we uphold high standards in our own life will trust us and want to do business with us in the future.

6. Integrity brings respect into our own lives

*It's been said that the more things a man is
ashamed of, the more respectable he is.*

Another great feature that upholding a life of integrity will bring is admiration from those who appreciate such values. As mentioned in the beginning of this chapter, everyone has an inner desire to be respected by others. *The best way to gain this respect is to be a person who maintains the qualities that are recognized in every society as honorable.* These include such virtues as honesty, kindness, faithfulness, and truthfulness. When we live with these qualities, others will automatically sense that we can be trusted. This is a major advantage in building wholesome relationships both on and off the job. Our friendships will have more depth simply because of the trust factor that integrity brings. Our relationship with customers will also be more connected simply because they too can sense that we are trustworthy enough to take care of their needs in a highly professional manner.

7. Integrity allows us to become more insightful

Right is right, even if everyone is against it,
and wrong is wrong, even if everyone is for it.
- William Penn

Another benefit of living a life marked by integrity is in the way it allows us to make wiser decisions each day. Our choices in life become more beneficial to both others and ourselves. Because life is filled with daily decisions, living with integrity will give us the best advantage in making the right choices. *We will tend to be more insightful because of the principles that are now guiding our decisions*. This will also benefit those we serve because of the way we handle each situation in a professional and clear-minded way. Also, our personal choices away from work will only enhance our performance when we are back on the job.

8. Integrity makes us trustworthy

Men of genius are admired, men of wealth are envied, men of power are feared, but only men of character are trusted.
- Unknown

Living a life guided by wholesome principles will also give others a reason to trust us. Think of those in your own life who have earned your trust. More than likely it is because they are dependable, truthful, and have honest principles. This will be the same for our customers.

They will consistently give us higher marks when we can be trusted. Without trust, customers will more than likely not return. *This is why building trust with those we serve must be at the forefront of every dentistry customer service campaign. When our customers have confidence in us, we in turn will be rewarded with their loyalty.* This allegiance can only occur when we have earned the trust and respect of those we serve.

9. Yesterdays are never regretted when we have integrity

A final point on the benefit of living a life of integrity is that our yesterdays are filled with few regrets. When we are guided by admirable principles, we can look back and know that we have lived a life with no regrets. Sorrows and disappointments are not a part of our past because of the virtues that have guided us along the way. We have no memories that need to be continually suppressed. On the contrary, we can gladly look back because of the right choices that our principles had directed us to make.

How can we be more respectful?

By now I hope it has become clear that being able to respect others is an outcome of maintaining self-respect in our own lives. When we walk with integrity, we will have very little difficulty in showing others respect. As I have learned from those whom I regard as having an attitude of respect, I observed ten qualities that reflect their lives. The following traits will help in building a more respectful attitude toward others.

Building a respectful attitude tip #1...
Have a high regard for others

I remember meeting a young man from the south that impressed me from the start by his well-behaved manners. This man had a great habit of showing respect to everyone he met. His mannerisms and demeanor toward others were outstanding. He simply had a way about himself that attracted others. *When I look back at this man's behavior, it becomes crystal-clear that he had a high regard for everyone that he met. His obvious politeness and tone of voice drew people in because of the way he honored them with his respectful attitude.*

Having a high regard for our customers will have the same effect if we understand that every human being deserves to be treated with dignity. Like the young man who showed courtesy to everyone he met, we too can learn to be this way toward others. Whether it is a customer coming in our doors or a neighbor down the street, being respectful will naturally happen more frequently if we learn to value each person as being important. Every person came into the world the same way. When we begin to see the true worth of individuals, we will improve on treating them with respect. Learning to have a high regard for others will transform our behavior into one of kindness, admiration, and respect.

Building a respectful attitude tip #2...
Learn to encourage others

Another great way to build a respectful attitude is to learn to encourage others. *If we are to be more honoring toward others it is paramount that we learn to support people with our words and actions.* In my own experiences I have found that those who have a consistent attitude of respect encourage others. They also attract others by their positive way of giving a thoughtful word at the right time. Respectful people have a way of making others feel better because of their encouraging support. Very rarely will we find words of discouragement come from a person who respects others. *They understand the power of words and choose them carefully.*

When we are with a person who has an attitude of respect, we are more inclined to be on our best behavior. *Respectful people also understand the strength that an encouraging word brings.* I believe that more words of affirmation would take place if we truly understood the power of words. We will be discussing in more detail this attitude in the next chapter. But for now, remember that a word of encouragement will go a long way in showing others respect.

Building a respectful attitude tip #3…
See the potential in others

*See others not as they are, but what
they can become.*

If we want to build a more respectful attitude toward others, we need to see each person's potential. Showing others respect simply means that we value them as a human being just like ourselves. We are no better or no worse. In my own life, I have had people who believed that I could improve or become something more. I cannot tell you how much I have respected them for seeing something that I did not recognize at the time. This is the beauty of showing others respect. *It allows people to pick themselves up and believe that they can move forward.* Our respectful attitude also gives a person a sense of dignity. When we see the potential in others, they in turn begin to stand taller. This is the positive power of respecting others.

Because life can be filled with peaks and valleys, it is important to keep in mind that we can never truly know where people are at in their own life. This is why prejudices and critical attitudes are detrimental in building healthy relationships. Not only do these attitudes keep us from being respectful, but also a judgmental attitude makes others uncomfortable in our presence. As service representatives, our first duty is to create a warm and welcoming atmosphere for each customer. If we want to create an accepting environment, it is important to look through the eyes of grace and see the potential in others.

Building a respectful attitude tip #4...
Learn to be pliable

> *You can accomplish by kindness what
> you cannot by force.*
> - Publilius Syrus

Having an attitude of respect toward others means that we do not have to always have our own way. Learning to respect the opinion of others and not demanding our own way all of the time is a quality found in respectful people. Being courteous means allowing others to make decisions without sulking. It's being pliable and allowing other people to make the choice. *When a person always has to have it his or her own way, others will feel disrespected because their opinion was not considered.* It would be like a few friends going out for pizza and the same person always insisted on mushrooms without considering that the others may not care for them. What this conveys is a sign of disrespect because their opinions were not regarded. If we always insist on our own way, we will soon find very few people wanting to join us for pizza.

Learning to be pliable on the job is critical if we are to get along with our co-workers. When we continually demand that things be done our way, we are expressing that we do not care about what others may think. In leadership this can be deadly for building a great dentistry customer service staff. Excellent managers are flexible and allow co-workers to openly share ideas on how to improve the overall operation. *Being pliable is a great way to show that we truly respect the opinion of others.*

Building a respectful attitude tip #5...
Respect yourself first

Earlier I shared on integrity and how it creates self-respect in our own life. *The first building block in being respectful toward others is having self-respect.* When we live by such virtues as honesty and integrity, our life will begin to manifest self-respect because we have nothing to conceal. The way we present ourselves to the outside world matches what we are in our private lives. *Nothing brings about self-respect faster.*

Whenever I meet someone who consistently conveys a respectful attitude toward others, I cannot help but imagine that they are governed by admirable virtues. This is what makes them respectful in the first place. *The benefit of living with admirable qualities is that it produces self-respect within us.* On the other hand, when we live with qualities that are less admirable, we will tend to lose self-respect. This is why it becomes difficult to respect others. How can we give what we do not have? In terms of serving others, the virtues that we live by will carry over in how well we take care of our customers.

Building a respectful attitude tip #6…
Learn to be considerate

Be the kind of friend you would want to have.

Being considerate toward others is a genuine sign that a person has an attitude of respect. As dentistry customer service representatives, our duty should be to consistently show consideration toward others. This is just common sense. It is difficult to be respectful when we are inconsiderate. Learning to modify this must begin with a change in attitude. *I have found that those who consistently provide outstanding service are well mannered and thoughtful in the way they treat others.* This alone has a major impact in how customers perceive the service. People will always make their first judgment of our organization by how well they have been treated. It can make all the difference in creating customer loyalty.

Building a respectful attitude can happen if we begin to be aware of how we treat others. Do we show kindness and listen to what is being said? Are we patient with a request? We may also want to be aware of our tone of voice when speaking. Do we convey a voice that is obliged to help, or one that expresses a feeling of impatience? These are little indications that will help us to see where improvements may need to take place. The more we examine our behavior toward others, the better off we will be in providing outstanding service.

Building a respectful attitude tip #7...
Train our tongue

Great minds talk about ideas; Average minds talk about things; Small minds talk about other people.
-Unknown

The power of words can have a profound affect on the way we relate to others. Our verbal communication can nurture as well as injure. *When we converse with others, the choice of words and how we express them will show others the level of respect that we have for them.* This is especially true when relating with our customers. Does our facial expression and tone of voice convey that we genuinely want to help them, or do they sense by our communication that we are just doing our job? Using the right words and backing them up with a pleasant tone of voice is one of the most important ways we can communicate that we are happy to serve our customers.

In order to develop an attitude of respect, we must allow our words to be respectful toward others. *Course jokes, rude comments, and bad language will quickly convey to others that we are not very respectful. When we use inappropriate language, it expresses to our listeners that we have little self-respect.* Our customers will also pick up on the choice of words we use. In order to present ourselves in a professional manner, it is essential that we speak words that are appropriate. Our customers will appreciate our proper choice of words and will walk away sensing that we have shown them respect.

CHAPTER 5

Building a respectful attitude tip #8...
Allow others the freedom to make choices

If I ever decide to write a book on parenting, one of the main points made would be to allow children the freedom to grow and mature. I would stress the idea that when we give children an appropriate level of autonomy for their age, it conveys that we respect them as humans. This is important if we are to have healthy children who will one day grow up to become healthy adults. *(I like to tell my own children that one day they will grow wings and fly away.)* By training our kids and then trusting that they will make the right decisions later in life is conveying that we have allowed them to grow and mature. In the same way, we will always demonstrate to others our genuine respect by allowing them to be who they are and not what we think they should to be. This is called respecting another person's freedom.

This also holds true for our customers. If it were our preference, we would desire every customer to be perfect with zero demands. But we know that every customer is different. Some will come through our doors and be completely satisfied from the start. Others may enter our establishment and need more attention. Still others may come in and require even more assistance. The point is that we as service providers need to adjust and allow our customers the freedom to express their immediate needs to us. When we do this, we are displaying an attitude of respect because we are simply allowing people to freely communicate their wants to us without trying to tell them what we think they need. We are allowing them the freedom to choose.

Building a respectful attitude tip #9...
Learn to become user-friendly

People who honor others with respect also allow themselves to be more approachable. I like to call this being user-friendly. This is an important quality to have if we are to excel in providing excellent service. When our customers sense that we are easily approachable, they will be more likely to rate our service on a higher level. The best way to become user-friendly is to express right from the start a genuine respect for every customer who we will have the pleasure to serve. When customers take note of our pleasant attitude and friendly disposition, they will feel more comfortable to approach us with any additional needs or questions.

Learning to be more approachable to our customers will happen when we honor them by being pleasant and kind. We can show this by expressing a friendly smile and a warm greeting. It is the little gestures that we convey that will give them the green light to approach us. It is our job to make them feel that we are there for them and happy to serve. When customers feel secure enough to approach us and ask for additional help, we can be sure that we have created a user-friendly environment for them.

Building a respectful attitude tip #10…
Listening conveys respect

In the last chapter on developing a caring attitude, I went into detail on the importance of listening to others. When we give our full attention, we are expressing a respectful attitude because it conveys that the person we are listening to is important enough to be heard. The power of undivided attention will allow others to express themselves. It also shows that we are considerate. Listening is so much more important than speaking. I frequently say that I never learn anything when I am talking. It is only in listening that true learning can occur. Observe conversations and take note of how much listening actually occurs in the course of a dialogue. It is always astonishing to notice how little is spent on actually listening. From my own observations, I have rarely witnessed one person asking another person a pertinent question during the course of the discussion. *Most of the conversation is focused primarily on statements being thrown back and forth with little inquiry on what had just been said.*

It is a joy to be in the presence of a person who truly is interested in listening. It is like finding a diamond in the rough. Listeners are a

Chapter 5

special breed and a pleasure to converse with. They not only make us feel special, but also allow us to express ourselves in a more meaningful way. *I have observed that it is the listeners of the world who tend to show others the most respect simply because they are not interested in having the spotlight on themselves.* They show respect by allowing the other person to speak. Remember this and others will soon appreciate the respect that you convey to them through your great listening skills!

♥

The Attitude of

Encouraging

Cheer, support, give confidence, persuade, reassure, strengthen, uplift, fortify, inspire, help.

Chapter 6

The Attitude of Encouraging

Encouragement creates a positive environment for both the customer and the company.

There is an attitude that can influence and help others to become their best. This attitude has the power to build people up. When we live with this attitude, not only will we make a positive difference in our environment, but also assist in bringing out the natural gifts of those around us. The influence that this attitude has on people will give strength and hope to move forward. No other attitude can assist in helping to bring out the best in others quite like this attitude. The attitude I am talking about is encouragement.

How many times have we been in the presence of a person who had a way of bringing out our best? What is it that brought out our finest behavior? More than likely, we were in the presence of a person who had the ability to encourage us either through words or actions. He or she had a way of making us feel better because of their gift of being able to encourage. They were inspirational and looked beyond what we presently were to what we could become. Their genuine care and concern made us realize that their kind words were authentic and without ulterior motives. There were no hidden agendas connected with their encouraging remarks. We knew that this person was honorable and sincere in their words.

When we truly begin to appreciate what encouragement can do for people, we will want to do it more often. *I am convinced that every one of us needs to be encouraged from time to time.* A positive word can lift people up and help them to become their best. Using words that build up instead of tear down can make all the difference in a person's life. Words have the power of life and death. The old saying that *"sticks and stones will break my bones but words will never harm me"* has been found to be untrue. Our words can hurt others and tear them down. Every day we have the choice to support others with our choice of words. We can be used as instruments to lift others up or put them down.

When we are serving customers, our words *(along with the tone of our voice)* can make all the difference in how they perceive our service. I have found that the service superstars have a way of communicating in a pleasant tone of voice. Their encouraging attitude and kind words instantly give us the confidence that they are looking out for our best interest. But what about those experiences where the service was marked with a dentistry customer service representative who showed no signs of encouragement. I can recall experiences where there would be no friendly greeting or welcoming smile offered. If anything, I felt that I was intruding on their time. There would be no positive sign of encouragement on their part. As a customer I wanted to leave as soon as possible. *Looking back, I can see that these not so pleasant dentistry customer service experiences were caused by a lack of encouragement and support.*

> *What men and women need is encouragement.... Instead of always harping on a man's faults, tell him of his virtues. Try to pull him out of his rut of bad habits.*
> --Eleanor H. Porter (Pollyanna)

If encouragement can help to bring the best out in others, why do we generally have a difficult time doing it? What keeps us from being more encouraging to others? If sincere encouragement is supposed to be proper and helpful, why is it so difficult to show? After much thought, I believe that encouragement is a gift that some are naturally born with; however, those without the gift of encouragement can develop it over time. In the first case scenario, there are some people who have been wonderfully gifted with the attitude of bringing out the

Chapter 6

best in others. From the start they have had a way of building people up with little or no thought as to what they are doing it. Encouraging others comes as natural as waking up in the morning. But then there are those who have learned over time the importance of inspiring others and have implemented it into their lives. This should give each of us hope that we can develop a better attitude that brings inspiration to others who may need a helping hand. Before we focus on the traits that will help us to become better encouragers, let's first look at what encouragement can do for others.

The benefits of encouraging

Correction does much, but encouragement will do more.

Over the years I have come to the conclusion that encouragement is the most efficient way to bring the best out in others. I am not talking about empty flattery or saying words that have ulterior motives connected with them. Sincere encouragement has no strings attached. It is important to note that encouraging others can be easily conveyed without a word spoken. It can be a sincere smile or a kind gesture that somehow conveys a feeling that we are on their side. When serving others, it is not so much the words that we use that will express to a person that we are behind them. In many ways it is the way we look at them, or the way we communicate with a friendly gesture that expresses a sense that we are there for them. Something as simple as a pleasant smile will bring encouragement. A friendly hand gesture will also express that we are pleased to see them. Using these small signs will consistently convey to our customers that we care.

Think about the importance of encouraging children during their early formative years. When children have parents or caretakers who understand the importance of encouragement, these children will have a big advantage in their future lives. I have witnessed children who came from homes where words of encouragement were freely given. The parents understood the power of encouragement and it showed in the lives of the children. On the other hand, I have sadly witnessed homes where the normal conversations were embedded with discouraging words and speech that tended to be dispiriting. This of course had an adverse effect in bringing out the best in everyone. In the same manner, if we rarely use words of encouragement, we will have a difficult time bringing out the best in others.

One word or a pleasant smile is often enough to lift a person up who simply needed encouragement.

Encouraging words are said to be what sunshine is to flowers. It can be compared to what water is to a man who has just walked twenty miles in a hot desert. To encourage another person is comparable to helping someone who has just fallen to the ground. It shows people that we are there for them and desire that they become their best. Without encouragement, people can slowly wilt like a flower with no water. *When we share a word of affirmation, it is as if we were lending an invisible hand.* With encouragement, there will be times when the results can be instantly seen. It can make a person stand a little taller and walk away with a slight smile on his or her face. A kind word spoken may be all that another person needed to lift them back up and begin afresh.

Eleven traits commonly found in an attitude of encouragement

We begin to blossom by an encouraging word, but slowly wilt without it.

1. Encouragers support others to be their best

Kind words can be short and easy to speak, but their echoes are truly endless.

The first characteristic found in those who have the gift of encouragement is their ability to bring out the best in others. *This is why encouragers make excellent leaders. They have a way of making others perform at their best.* When we encounter someone who simply loves to encourage, it makes us want to be and do our best. We are attracted to the fact that they believe in

CHAPTER 6

us. This one single point becomes a powerful motivator for us to be our absolute best in their presence. It is almost as if we would not want to disappoint them by not trying our best or being on our best behavior. In terms of serving others, *our encouraging attitude will have a positive effect in bringing out their "best customer side" and give them the desire to present their best.* This is because encouragement will always have a way of bringing out the best in everyone, including our customers.

2. Encouragers rarely complain

Those who are lifting the world upward and onward are those who encourage more than criticize.

Think of people who you consider to be great at encouraging others. If you examine their lives more closely, you will notice that they very seldom complain. Encouragers are encouragers because they consistently see the good side of every situation. Instead of seeing the cloudy day, encouragers point to the blue skies behind the clouds. If we are to be better at encouraging others, our first priority is to get rid of all forms of complaining. Not only does grumbling put a monkey wrench in the way we view life, but it also can make us unattractive to be around. How many of us actually enjoy being around those who constantly complain about this and that? Complaining also has a way of making us less encouraging toward others. *The people who encourage can do so because they have learned that whining and faultfinding eventually bring only discontentment into their lives.* If we want to be more encouraging, the first priority is to catch ourselves when we want to grumble and replace it with a heart that is thankful.

3. Encouragers are sincere in their compliments

Flatter me, and I may not believe you. Criticize me, and I may not like you. Encourage me, and I will not forget you.

Sincerity is the true mark of a person who genuinely encourages others. Being able to compliment another person with no ulterior motive is the distinctive feature of genuine encouragement. These people are not afraid to offer a kind word to another person. This is one of the best qualities that an attitude of encouragement has. When we compliment others in sincerity we are presenting them a gift. *But if our compliments are artificial and insincere, it conveys to people nothing more than empty flattery with hidden strings attached.* This of course should never happen. To expect something in return for an admiring comment given is detrimental to any relationship. *The rule of thumb is never to expect anything in return for a kind word given to another.* By being sincere and honest in offering compliments, we will convey that we genuinely care for those we are encouraging.

4. Encouragers are out to help others

The best help that we can render an afflicted man is not to take away his burden, but to lend him a shoulder, that he may be able to bear the burden.

Of all the positive traits that an encouraging attitude conveys to others, none is more powerful than the impression that we are out to help them. When people sense that we want the best for them, not only will they flourish, but they will also open up and trust us more. In delivering outstanding service to our customers, they will appreciate the feeling that we genuinely want to help them. Customers who sense our sincere desire to give them the best possible service will have all the more confidence in our ability to take care of their needs. They in turn will become loyal and trust our future judgments simply because they know that we care.

A word of encouragement during a failure is worth more than an hour of praise after success.

When we simply want to help others without any ulterior motive, they in turn may eventually become loyal in return. This can be explained by the positive influence of a caring heart. When we care for others, they may automatically begin to care for us. When we want to help others, they in turn want to help us. *In essence, we can sum it up by saying that others will eventually treat us the way that we have treated*

Chapter 6

them. When we treat our customers with such attributes as kindness, caring, and respect, we will find that they will desire to do the same.

5. Encouragers urge others to better themselves

When we seek to discover the best in others, we somehow bring out the best in ourselves.
- William Arthur Ward

Another excellent characteristic that we can find in people who encourage is their ability to persuade others to better themselves. *Encouragers see not what people are but what they can become.* When they converse with another person, they begin to recognize untapped qualities that the person may never have recognized. It is as if these encouragers are gifted with the ability to see the potential in others.

Children learn more from models than from critics.

If we are to improve at encouraging others, we must look beyond what someone is at the present moment and see what he or she can become. By doing this, we will begin to see others in a different light. People will be drawn to us simply because of our accepting attitude. It is as if we are giving them the confidence and conviction that they can change for the better. Where they may have been on the verge of giving up, our encouraging words begin to allow them to have the courage to continue. This is the power of giving encouragement to others.

6. Encouragers are secure in who they are

When we are secure and confident in who we are, we are much more inclined to encourage others. The reason for this is that self-assurance allows us the freedom to build others up without wanting the spotlight on ourselves. *Encouragers are confident enough within themselves to pick others up with kind words or a helping hand.* On the other hand are those who try to criticize or put others down in an attempt to feel better about themselves. This self-destructive behavior is an indication that the person is dealing with hidden insecurities. Secure people have no need to judge or speak poorly of others in order to lift themselves up. On the contrary, people who enjoy lifting others up exhibit a self-confidence that allows this to occur. In reality, it is the encouragers of the world who are most secure in whom they are. That is why they have no need to criticize others. This will play a positive role in our relationship with others. *Remember, the more secure a person is, the more likely he or she will be able to freely encourage others.*

7. Encouragers never stop growing

Those who bring sunshine into the lives of others cannot keep it from themselves.

Another trait that we will find in people who encourage is their desire to continue to learn. Because of their desire to see others reach their full potential in life, they carry this conviction into their own personal lives. This desire to see others grow is a benefit that will motivate an encourager to become his or her best. This aspiration to learn is a characteristic that identifies those who enjoy building others up. *Without realizing it, they have developed a healthy inner drive to better themselves simply because their outward attitude of encouraging others has positively affected them!* When we truly see the potential in others, we cannot help but want to use our gifts and talents to the best of our ability. This is the reason that people with an attitude of encouragement continue to grow. Their desire to help others has motivated their own lives.

8. Encouragers are excited when others achieve

We need to applaud the accomplishments of others, recognize their successes, and encourage them in their pursuits. By helping others, everybody wins.

Those who have a genuine attitude of encouragement express joy when others achieve a certain goal or accomplishment. Because of their good nature, encouragers carry no jealousy or insecurities. *They are happy when people succeed and are not threatened by the triumphs and successes of others.* When our attitude is one where we can rejoice in the victories of others, we can be confident that we are self-secure within ourselves. Because of the self-confidence that goes along with an encouraging attitude, these people are secure enough to not have to compare themselves with others. Being secure with who they are, they do not feel better about themselves when others fail or fall short of a goal. *On the contrary, they enjoy seeing others succeed. This is the true sign of someone who genuinely has the gift of encouragement.* Another benefit is that it makes people want the encourager to succeed as well. Because encouragers never show jealousy or animosity, others cannot help but want the best for them.

9. Encouragers attract like magnets

The most helpful, influential, and predictable people-builders are praise and encouragement.

When we consistently live a lifestyle of encouraging others, we will begin to notice that our friendships will take on more depth. Similar to the gift of listening, people will begin to open up simply because of our supportive personality. Not only will we be an encouragement, but we will also notice others wanting to be an encouragement to us. Think about those in your own life who have been friendly and supportive. How did that make you feel? More than likely you were drawn in by their helpful and encouraging words. It works with our customers as well. Our encouraging attitude toward them will not only enhance their overall experience, but also attract them back time and again. What our customers appreciate is how we have taken the time to be caring and helpful. They cannot help but appreciate the consideration that we have shown.

10. Encouragers take their eyes off themselves

One of the best attributes of having an attitude of encouragement is that it takes our eyes off ourselves and puts them on others. Being an encourager toward others allows us to focus our attention away from ourselves. *It makes us less self-centered simply because we are not continually attempting to get others to pay attention to us.* People who tend to be self-absorbed have a difficult time encouraging because giving genuine encouragement never seeks attention. As mentioned earlier in the chapter, encouragers can support others freely because of their inner security. This is why the encouragers of the world are not threatened by the achievements of others. *They do not determine who they are by measuring the success or failures of others in comparison to their own accomplishments.* Being self-confident, the encouragers enjoy celebrating the triumphs of others without having their own self-worth threatened. This also is why they can freely give others encouragement. When a person can genuinely compliment others, it is an indication that they are self-assured with who they are.

11. Encouragers are rarely down

Having an attitude of encouragement has additional benefits that will also help us along the road of life. As we live a life that seeks to build others up, we will soon notice how others will want to lift us up as a result of our goodwill toward them. That is why encouragers rarely stay down for very long. Because of their desire to support and encourage, people in turn will want to do the same for them. I am convinced that the healthiest friendships are founded on two people building each other up. It becomes one of mutual support where each person wants nothing but the best for the other. With this kind of friendship, it is difficult to stay down because of the strength and support that encouragement brings.

It is also important to note that encouraging has a way of making others want to support us. When we care for others and desire the best for them, they in turn want to do all they can to help us. With this in mind, the best action we can take if we want healthy and caring friendships is to be caring ourselves. When we live a life of building others up, our friendships will be based more on mutual respect and admiration for the other person. This will also carry over in our relationship with customers. They will see that we are out to give them our best, and in return they will show their appreciate by becoming loyal to our organization.

CHAPTER 6

The secret of creating a great dentistry customer service team

By now I hope that we can understand the positive influences that encouragement has on other people. If we are to build a great dentistry customer service team, it is paramount that we create an environment where each member of the team is encouraged to do their best. *The best managers understand that positive reinforcement will always outperform negative words of discouragement.* When a leader leads with the best interest of others, he or she will continually offer words of encouragement. Instead of looking for little faults or minor mistakes, the best leaders have a way of communicating that consistently brings out the best in others. These managers have a way of relating to their team that both inspires and motivates each person to do their best. They use their words carefully and never come across in a rude or impolite manner. When managers consistently work toward bringing out the best in their team, the team will show their appreciation by doing their best on the job.

I am always baffled when hearing accounts where the leadership consistently uses dispiriting words in an effort to motivate those under them. In reality, this approach will only backfire for those who communicate in ill-mannered ways. *This is because people will never want to do their best when they have been disrespected. They may do what needs to be done to get the job finished, but their hearts will never be in it.*

On the other hand, when management genuinely cares about the welfare of those who work for them, the attitude of the environment will change for the better. When people are encouraged and treated in a manner that is both respectful and honoring, the responsibilities of the job will take on new meaning. This is the beauty of encouraging. *It gives employees the desire to want to do their best simply because they have been treated with dignity.* This also creates a work environment where everyone begins to build each other up. This positive atmosphere becomes a chain reaction that eventually will have an effect on the way our customers are treated. *Exceptional dentistry customer service then becomes a by-product and reflection of the way management has treated their employees.* This is the secret of creating a great dentistry customer service team.

♥

The Attitude of

Thankfulness

Grateful, thoughtfulness, appreciative, pleased, gratified, much obliged, praise, benediction, indebtedness.

Chapter 7

The Attitude of Thankfulness

*Customers who feel appreciated will rate
our service higher.*

One of the secrets for living a more fulfilling life is being able to consistently live with a heart of gratitude. There is something that changes our whole outlook on life when we capture the ability to appreciate the simple gift called life. No other attitude has a way of filling us with delight as does capturing the attitude of being thankful. Not only will it affect every area of our life, but it will also make us more attractive to be around. Being in the presence of those who are thankful can be comparable to a peaceful sunset across a calm lake. We watch as the sun slowly fades away and in complete silence we sense the beauty of it. In the same manner, when we are in the presence of someone who radiates appreciation for simply being alive, we silently sense the beauty that it portrays.

Thankfulness is never anything that we can buy or barter for. Just look into the lives of thousands of affluent people throughout the pages of history and we will discover that wealth has never brought lasting happiness. The reason for this is because contentment and gratitude grows within the quietness of our hearts. No amount of gold or silver will purchase it for us. Temporary treasures eventually fade and we begin to search again. I like to compare it to a man who is dying of thirst and begins to drink salt water from the sea. Before long he becomes thirsty again, but this time his thirst has increased all the more. In the same way, trying to capture a thankful heart by collecting material objects will eventually leave us wanting more.

> *To be content with little, difficult.*
> *To be content with much, impossible.*

So what does this have to do with dentistry customer service and being able to deliver outstanding service to our customers? How exactly does having a heart of appreciation connect with serving others? I believe it is one of the best attitudes that we can have for becoming dentistry customer service superstars. *When we truly live a life of appreciation, it will carry over in the way that we treat others, especially those we serve.* This is the advantage of living with a thankful heart. When we start to live with an attitude of gratitude, we will begin to improve in every other area of our life, including our service to others. But before moving on, it's important that we understand the customer's perspective when they are shown appreciation.

Why appreciation appeals to our customers

> *"Gratitude is not only the greatest of virtues,*
> *but the parent of all others."*
> -- Marcus Cicero

I remember coming across a story about a young man who had been fired from an ice cream parlor. One of his duties was to say thank you whenever he handed an ice cream cone to a customer. The owner of the parlor understood the power of appreciation and made it a part of the job description for each employee who served ice cream. The owner finally had to let the young man go because of his forgetfulness to say thank you.

I relate this story because I am convinced that customers will always rate our service higher if we show them our appreciation in having done business with us. I am also convinced that the organization that

Chapter 7

consistently shows appreciation will have an advantage over other similar businesses. We must remember that in today's economy one company can practically match another company's product. What can separate us from the pack is the service and the appreciation that we show. Here's an example. Let's say that I was to open a family restaurant, and the area already had eight similar restaurants. I am pretty sure that the food in each restaurant would all taste similar and the prices would all be competitive. *What I would focus on the most would be to hire people who had hospitable personalities. They would have to be welcoming and excited to be working at the restaurant. I would also look for the six attitudes described in this book. I would want them to be friendly, enthused, caring, respectful, encouraging, and thankful.*

If I could find people who had all of these qualities there would be no question that this new restaurant would be an instant hit. *Customers would want to come back simply because of the way that we made them feel.* More importantly, we would make it a habit to show each customer our sincere appreciation for visiting our restaurant. Before leaving, I would want to make sure every customer knew that we were thankful that they chose us over the other restaurants.

The power of appreciation can never be underestimated. Think of the times that we may have done something nice for someone and soon forgot about it. A few days later we receive a card in the mail with a note of appreciation for what we did. Taken by surprise, we feel overwhelmed that someone would take the time to actually send us a card. How did it make us feel? More than likely it felt good to have been appreciated. This gesture of appreciation also gave us an inner desire to want to help this person in the future. *In the same manner, when we show appreciation to our customers, they in turn want to support us.* We need to understand that everyone enjoys being appreciated. This is why having an attitude of thankfulness is so beneficial if we want to become dentistry customer service superstars.

A few years ago my wife and I surprised our three children at Christmas with a little puppy. He was a cute little fellow with fluffy white curls, and we named him Cuddles. It didn't take long for us to fall in love with Cuddles because of his loving ways. Anyone who has ever had a dog can relate to what I am saying. As I reflect on Cuddles, I have come to realize that one of his most likable traits is how he can display his appreciation toward us. When we take off to run errands, guess who is always waiting by the front window for our return? His excitement and appreciation in seeing us return can sometimes be overwhelming. With Cuddles jumping and wagging his tail at us, we cannot help but feel loved. It is this "secret weapon" of being thankful that has won our utmost loyalty to our little dog.

Like Cuddles, we too can win the hearts of our customers when we show them how much we appreciate their support. Unlike Cuddles, we do not have to jump up and down when we welcome our customers, *but how about giving a friendly and hospitable greeting to convey how much we appreciate that they have decided to do business with us?* This small gesture of showing our customers appreciation is without question one of the best things we can offer them. But remember that expressing thankfulness must be sincere and from the heart. I am sure that you can recall moments as a customer when you were given a somewhat expressionless thank-you that did not seem real. *More than likely it was spoken out of duty versus out of the heart.*

The worst poverty is produced by a life empty of gratitude.

The two types of thank-you

I have found that the expression of thank-you given after being served by a dentistry customer service representative falls under two basic categories. The first category is when service representatives express a thank-you simply because it falls under their job description. *This type of thank-you is usually forgotten before the customer reaches the exit door.* As customers, we can easily spot this thank-you because of the way it was expressed and the lack of genuineness conveyed. It would be similar to the tone of voice received if we were to ask where the restrooms were located. The second category of receiving a thank-you is much more attractive because of its sincerity. *We as customers can sense through the pleasant tone of voice and appreciative smile that this expression was sincere.* When this occurs, we walk away feeling like kings and queens. The power of sincere appreciate toward others not only attracts, but it also makes people want to continue to support us. Once we truly understand this, we will see more customers knocking on our doors.

Staying away from complaining

"What if you gave someone a gift, and they neglected to thank you for it — would you be likely to give them another? Life is the same way. In order to attract more of the blessings that life has to offer, you must truly appreciate what you already have."
-- Ralph Marston - Writer

One of the best benefits of having an attitude of gratitude is that it not only gives others a good feeling inside, but also makes us healthier. Thankfulness has a way of keeping us overflowing with inner delight. I have found that those who are most content in life are people who consistently show appreciation. On the other side are those who give the impression of never being content. Their most prevalent attitude tends to be one of complaining. Not only are they rarely satisfied about most things, but they also show little appreciation toward others. I believe that the main reason that it is difficult for these complainers to show thankfulness is because of the constant grumbling that has eroded any signs of joy. *When we begin to moan and complain, we will soon find that it becomes more difficult to appreciate life. Grumbling has a way of whittling away a thankful heart.* Complaining has to be the number one roadblock for obtaining an attitude of appreciation. No other attitude can destroy us like complaining.

The best antidote for staying away from a complaining attitude is to simply avoid it altogether. I realize this suggestion sounds too straightforward, but the only thing that will continue to feed this destructive attitude is to continue to do it. Complaining may start small and innocently, but over time it can affect every other attitude. I believe it needs to be avoided like the plague. Nothing good will ever come when we live a life of constant complaining.

Eight benefits of a thankful attitude

"In our daily lives, we must see that it is not happiness that makes us grateful, but the gratefulness that makes us happy."

1. Thankful people treasure life

   The best things in life are not things.

Of all the benefits that are given to those with a thankful attitude, none is as priceless as being able to simply appreciate the gift we call life. Those who have developed a heart of gratitude enjoy life on a much more grander scale. They see through a different set of lenses because being thankful has allowed them to take in every day as a gift to be treasured. *When we cultivate a heart of thankfulness, we are then able to see life as a moment-by-moment experience. We neither dwell on the past nor fret about the future. Our outlook becomes one where each day is all we have, and for this we are grateful.*

On the other hand, if we have not learned to appreciate life we will have a difficult time being grateful for the other things that come our way. In chapter two I briefly shared about survivor stories and the attitude of enthusiasm for life that came as a result of those who were rescued. *In the same way, we can have this same appreciation if we will only realize that life is a gift and the only true way to enjoy it is by being thankful.* Those who have survived ship wrecks and POW camps come out with a new perspective on life. We can have this attitude as well if we will only stop and consider how quickly life passes by.

When we have this outlook on life, we will begin to treat others with such virtues as kindness, respect, and thankfulness. *Our service to others will be more than just following a job description. It will start to be a way to express our appreciation for life.* We will eventually see ourselves being more patient with people and giving them our best service. Along with this we will begin to attract others simply because of the appreciation that radiates from within. *The benefit of seeing life as a gift is indeed one of the greatest gifts that we can give ourselves.*

2. Thankful people are contented people

> *It is the nature of desire not to be satisfied.*
> - Aristotle

When I look at all six attitudes that we have discussed so far, *I cannot imagine a state of mind that will bring more contentment into our lives than having the attitude of thankfulness.* No other outlook will bring us to a place of happiness quite like appreciation. If we think about it, everyone is seeking contentment. We buy this product and that gadget with the hope that it will satisfy our craving to be happy. Soon we discover that the automobile we were so excited to purchase is starting to show rust near the bottom of the door. The outfit we couldn't wait to wear soon finds its way into the Salvation Army bag.

In our pursuit for contentment we find that the excitement soon wears out, and off we go again looking for the next gadget or experience that will give us instant gratification. *Could it be that we have stopped being grateful for the little things? If this is the case, maybe it is time to stop and ask ourselves if the problem could be that we've stopped being thankful for the simple gift of life.* When this occurs we start to find it difficult to appreciate almost anything. Once we rediscover the benefits of having an attitude of thankfulness, we will then begin to slow down our search for things that we believed would finally bring us contentment. *We will find that things can never bring the contentment that an attitude of gratitude delivers time and again.*

3. Thankful people attract others

The secret to contentment is not measured in what we possess, but by the amount of thankfulness that resides in our hearts. This alone makes us attractive to those who are searching.

Earlier I briefly shared how thankfulness has a way of attracting others. The reason for this is because in the heart of every person is a search for contentment. Deep inside we know that being thankful is an admirable trait. We also sense that becoming a grateful person would make us happier. *What we tend to forget is that our life continually needs to be seen as a gift that should be treasured.* When we understand this we can begin to learn to complain less and appreciate more.

Thankful people have a way of attracting others because of their contented ways. The trappings of the world do not allure those who live with gratitude. They have no need to keep searching for something to make them content. *They have found that the secret to contentment is not measured in what they possess, but by the amount of thankfulness that resides in their hearts. This alone makes these people attractive to those who are continually searching.*

If I were to pinpoint one attitude that would make a person instantly more attractive, it would have to be thankfulness. When we genuinely are thankful to be alive and consider life as a gift, our whole outlook begins to change. We would naturally smile more. Our daily lives would be filled with more laughter, and we would begin to appreciate the little things that were once overlooked. Our wonderment for life would be comparable to a small child who observes a picture of a giraffe for the first time. In amazement he takes in the whole experience and is fully engulfed in what he is seeing. In similar fashion, our enthusiasm will begin to overtake us because of the thankfulness we have for simply being alive. It would be like visiting the local zoo and observing a giraffe for the first time.

Chapter 7

When we truly appreciate life, we will automatically improve in our service to others. We will want to help others because we begin to see that fulfillment comes from serving. By doing this, others will take notice and sense something different in us. They will be attracted to our caring ways and take notice of our appreciative attitude. This will also help in building stronger relationships both on and off the job. People will be attracted to our non-selfish ways and want to know what it is that makes us tick.

4. Thankful people avoid complaining

The squeaking wheel doesn't always get the grease. Sometimes it gets replaced.

One of the most telling signs of a thankful person is the lack of complaining that goes on in his or her life. As mentioned earlier, grumbling is the number one enemy in cultivating a heart of gratefulness. When we live with an outlook of appreciation and gratitude, our life becomes more fulfilling. We will learn to overlook little offenses that may come our way. We will also begin to see the positive characteristics of others and treat them with respect. Our relationships will be more cheerful because of the changes that thankfulness has brought into our lives.

The problem with complaining is that it changes the way we view life. Our vision becomes distorted in that we begin to see what is wrong with the world. Bellyaching makes us less friendly to be around because of our negative outlook on life. Instead of seeing the good in others, we begin looking for the little faults. This of course soon becomes detrimental in how well we serve others. Complaining will affect every aspect of life, not the least being our attitude. If we are to serve others with pleasure, it is paramount that we learn to catch ourselves when we fall into a grumbling attitude. *This will guard us from losing our appreciation for life. By staying away from complaining and faultfinding, we will soon discover one of the best antidotes for living a life of thankfulness.*

5. Thankful people are kindhearted

When we begin to appreciate life, we will start to treat others with more kindness and consideration.

Think of the people in your life who always tend to be thankful. Their daily lives reflect appreciation and gratitude. *Another great feature that you will notice in these thankful people is their kindness toward others.* Becoming more thoughtful toward others is another benefit of living a life with an attitude of thankfulness. When we begin to appreciate life, we will also start to treat others with more kindness and consideration. Appreciation has a way of also changing the way we act toward others. We will begin to see such virtues as gentleness and patience appear in our relationships. Living a life of thankfulness begins to bring out the best of who we are and how we treat others.

In order to improve in our relationship with customers, it is essential that we consistently show appreciation. As mentioned earlier, everyone enjoys being appreciated. This is especially true in the lives of those we serve. In today's economy, the consumer has many choices. Today's customer can pick from six golf courses, seven barbershops, eight pizzerias, and nine auto repair shops. Because the first five minutes of contact with a company is critical in whether the customer will return, it is important to show consideration from the start. This is because the very first judgment that will be made on the service being provided is how friendly the people were. When we have employees who have attitudes of thankfulness, benevolence toward others will naturally flow. *This first impression will have a major influence in bringing new customers back time and again.*

6. Thankful people have healthier friendships

When we live a life of appreciation, our friendships will have much more substance. Others will enjoy our company simply because of our attractive outlook on life. They will sense our thankful hearts and want it in their own lives. This of course is another benefit of being thankful. Not only will it affect the way we live each day, but it will make positive changes in other people as well. The old saying that states "birds of a feather flock together" holds true. Thankful people tend to attract thankful people. This is also true for those who live with a complaining attitude. Complainers have a way of attracting other complainers into their circle of friends.

Being grateful allows us to build healthier relationships. We appreciate others more and they in turn enjoy being around us. It becomes a win-win situation. *When we genuinely appreciate people, they cannot help but be attracted to the fact that we are thankful for them. This is why living with an attitude of thankfulness brings healthier relationships into our lives.* The more we appreciate others, the more others will enjoy our company. On the other hand, if we are always grumbling, we will soon find ourselves alone with few friends around to support us.

In serving others, customers will naturally be drawn to our appreciative attitude. They cannot help but sense how much gratitude permeates from us. This will also allow us to excel in our work environment. Other co-workers will enjoy our company because of our grateful attitude. This also will make the work atmosphere more positive and help to create a better service team.

7. Thankful people are more understanding

Living a life of thankfulness allows us to be more understanding toward others. This is another benefit of living with appreciation. *We become more patient and accepting of others because of our lack of faultfinding.* We begin to show others more grace without having to point out every minor blunder that we may notice. Our thankfulness allows us to see others with a less critical attitude. We learn to overlook minor flaws and instead notice the admirable strengths and good points of people.

One of the best gifts that we can offer our customers is patience. This is because the customer is essentially asking for help. *Because they are in a vulnerable position of seeking assistance, we can make them feel more at ease by simply showing patience.* Within no time the customer will feel more comfortable because we are not giving them the impression that they are taking up our time. When customers sense that they are not an interruption, they in turn will rate our level of service much higher.

8. Thankful people have a life filled with color

When we live with thankfulness, our world becomes more colorful. Reds become richer, greens become grander, and blues become brighter. *Instead of the dull black and white lives of those who live with a grumbling attitude, we are allowed to see the brilliance of living through the eyes of gratitude. Thankfulness has a way of making us see things differently.* Instead of seeing a pile of leaves on the lawn waiting to be raked, we now see the beauty that the fall colors bring our way. Instead of seeing the clouds in the sky, we now see the majestic blue skies in the background. *Such is the life in a day of a thankful heart!*

When we see the advantages of living with a heart of thankfulness, it becomes clear that this way of life is our only solid choice. If we look at the benefits that an attitude of gratitude brings into our lives, we would soon find that complaining, grumbling, whining, and faultfinding are simply not beneficial for living a well-balanced life.

God gave you a gift of 86,400 seconds today. Have you used one to say "thank you?"
- William Arthur Ward

Chapter 8

When Attitudes Go Astray

By now it should be obvious that every area of our life will be affected tremendously by how well we manage these six important attitudes both on and off the job. But what happens when one of the six attitudes goes astray? Is there a quick formula for getting back on track and changing an attitude that fell off course? These are legitimate questions that we will be tackling in the next chapter. But before we seek solutions, let's look at what happens when each attitude goes astray.

When friendliness goes astray

Over the years I have discovered that life operates much better when we are friendly toward others. Not only do we enhance our relationships, but also we will find other people becoming more courteous toward us. But what happens when the attitude of friendliness is lacking in a person? How do others begin to respond to those with unfriendly attitudes? The first thought that comes to mind is that living with an attitude of aloofness will make other people less amiable toward us. We will soon find people going out of their way to avoid us. As a customer, the service we receive from others will tend to be poor in response to the unfriendly attitude that we have shown.

Unfriendliness will also make us view the world differently. Instead of seeing the good points in people, our unkindness will tend to bring out the less desirable traits in others. *More than likely, people will respond to us in an unfavorable manner simply because of the unfriendliness that we have shown.* Eventually we may even come to the conclusion that everyone is discourteous and impolite. Our view of the world becomes distorted because of the ill-mannered behavior that we have projected. Being unfriendly will also make our friendships fragile. People will eventually have a difficult time putting up with our impolite manners. Only the abundantly patient friends will attempt to maintain any further contact. In the end, we will find that projecting an attitude of unfriendliness brings nothing but loneliness and a bleak outlook on everything that comes our way.

When enthusiasm goes astray

When we lose our attitude of enthusiasm, life tends to become boring and tiresome. Waking up in the morning takes longer. Every day becomes tedious and uninteresting. Without enthusiasm, our existence soon becomes one of just trying to get by. We eventually lose the zest for life and have nothing to anticipate in the future. This of course is no way to live.

It is interesting to note that a very similar occurrence happened in the POW camps. Those who survived the camps during war have written about fellow prisoners who did not make it out. One common theme is that they were able to tell who would and would not survive. Survivors have testified that the prisoners who eventually died in the camps would lose the will to live and withdraw from others. Many would simply give up and crawl into a corner waiting for the end to come. *In all of these cases, what always preceded death was a lack of will to live.* They simply had given up hope of surviving. I share this to point out that a loss of enthusiasm for life can have a similar effect on people outside the walls of a POW camp. A loss of enthusiasm can lessen our will to live. Comparable to the prisoners who simply lost their will to survive, our lack of enthusiasm for living can negatively affect our outlook on life.

I find it interesting to note that those who appear to be more excited about life also tend to live healthier lives. Their enthusiasm provides a more positive outlook and puts an extra spring in their steps. On the other hand, I also find it interesting to discover that a lack of enthusiasm can have the opposite effect on a person's life. Losing our excitement for living has no long-term benefits.

CHAPTER 8

When caring goes astray

*Caring about others is the cornerstone
of every other attitude.*

When we begin to care less about others, negative consequences begin to emerge in our lives. Similar to an unfriendly attitude, when we are uncaring our world begins to look desolate. Not only do we begin to lose close friendships, but we will also become more isolated from others. Because caring about others is the cornerstone of every other attitude that we project, becoming apathetic about life makes our world appear unwelcoming. *We also start to think that nobody cares, when in reality it is only a distortion that grew out of our indifference toward others.*

Caring is at the heart of who others perceive us to be. Every healthy relationship is based on mutual caring. When others sense that we genuinely care, they in turn will respond positively toward us. On the other hand, an uncaring attitude pushes people away. Whether we are serving customers or working with co-workers, our indifference toward them will hurt us in the end. Very few people will respond positively toward us. If anything, few will want to befriend us. This is due to our unwillingness to care. It eventually can isolate us from true friendships and a more fulfilling life. *Caring is one attitude that needs to be consistently maintained if we are to find the inner joy that thoughtfulness brings.*

When respect goes astray

*We bring out the best in others simply
by showing them respect.*

Showing proper respect toward every person has countless benefits. Not only will our relationships be enriched, but we will also be shown respect in return. Remember, what goes around comes around. *When we genuinely convey respect toward another person, it sends a message that they are important. For those who see the significance of every human being, offering respect becomes second nature.* Everyone appreciates being shown respect. Respecting others allows us to convey a measure of admiration. It shows people that we regard and esteem them. This type of attitude is proper and should be given high priority in every society. To show respect is just common courtesy that should consistently be expressed to others.

But what happens when respecting others goes astray? How can we relate and have meaningful relationships if we do not show proper honor to others? In all likelihood, the first area that will be affected is our relationships. It does not matter if we are talking about customers, co-workers, friends, or family members. *When we become disrespectful toward people, they in turn will think less of us. This is because we have conveyed to them through our disrespect that they are not important. Showing disrespect is the same as telling someone that they do not matter.* This antisocial behavior will turn others quickly away and create undesirable feelings. It does not matter the age or culture. When we are disrespecting others we are communicating that they have no significance. There is nothing good that can come from not showing other people respect. It is an attitude that should consistently be avoided.

When encouraging goes astray

There is something to be said about the encouragers of the world. They are always there to give a helping hand or offer a kind word. Their relationships with others are fulfilling because of their positive outlook on life. But what happens when our attitude shows little or no encouragement? What is the outcome of living a life where we rarely encourage others? More than likely we will find ourselves alone or surrounded with like-minded people who never build others up. If encouragement is lacking in our life, we will tend to see life in a more negative light.

Because 99.9% of encouragers see life in a more positive light, they will also be more optimistic. But what of those who rarely support others? More than likely they will live a pessimistic lifestyle. They will rarely congratulate a person when he or she has done something worth commending. If we are lacking in an attitude of encouraging, we will also have a difficult time complimenting others. We will keep to ourselves and rarely if ever pat a person on the back. Eventually we will surround ourselves with like-minded people who will only reflect our negative behavior. We also will find less compliments and encouraging words coming our way due to the gloomy attitude that we have entangled ourselves with.

When Thankfulness goes astray

The first sign that we are allowing an attitude of thankfulness to go astray is when we find ourselves complaining and grumbling. Nothing exposes an unappreciative heart quite as fast as murmuring about this or that. There is something attractive about a thankful heart. On the other hand, there is a drawback when complaining begins to take over our life. We start to lose a heart of thankfulness the moment we begin to grumble about something. *This is because having an attitude of gratitude cannot co-exist with a heart of complaining.* It is like mixing oil and water together.

If there is one attitude that needs to be guarded at all times, it is the attitude of gratitude. This brightens our whole outlook on life. But once we start to complain we begin to lose the joy that thankfulness gives. It is important to continually be aware when we begin to grumble. If left alone, it will eventually blind us to any sense of gratitude and begin to make us miserable.

Chapter 9

A Time to Improve

As we look back at all six attitudes, it should become apparent by now that our outlook on life will make all the difference in how we treat others. *The way that people perceive our service is influenced largely by the attitudes that we carry on the job.* We can have the best product on the market but lose customers simply because we do not make them feel welcomed. Every type of organization can begin to improve their dentistry customer service ratings if they understood that every business is first and foremost about people. In reality, it does not matter what type of organization we are talking about because customers are the reason for its existence. Everything from the little hotdog stand on the corner of a big city to the largest health insurance company in the world must focus on making their customers trust them enough to return in the future. Hopefully by now we can see that customer loyalty can only occur when we treat others with the attitudes discussed. As I have pondered on this idea of loyalty and what it takes to win a customer, I am convinced that it must start with maintaining all six attitudes that we have looked at.

Taking a personal inventory

I hope by now we can see the importance that our attitude plays in how well we conduct ourselves both on and off the job. *Our attitude can be said to be the key that unlocks our success in both our career and relationships.* How we succeed can be a direct link to the attitudes that we choose to embrace. We can live a life filled with qualities that can either attract or repel. Everyday we make personal choices in how we will relate to others. Ultimately it is our choice alone in how we will treat people. We can choose an attitude of friendliness, respect and appreciation. We can live a life that reflects that we care about people. In the end, it is our decision. No one can force us to be friendly or thankful. The choice is ultimately ours and ours alone.

With this thought in mind, the question begging to be asked is simply why would we not want to have the attitudes that will only enhance our lives? What true benefit does a sour attitude bring? In all honesty, choosing an attitude that repels others will only make us less attractive to be around. If we were to take a deep, long look and weigh the benefits of having a healthier attitude, the choice would become crystal clear. The advantages of treating others with such virtues as kindness, respect, and appreciation far outweigh having an attitude of unfriendliness, disrespect, and ingratitude. There truly are no comparisons.

Life begins to take on a whole new meaning when we start to appreciate and care about others. We will begin to notice that others treat us differently. I am reminded of the story of a friendly man who had recently moved to a new town. Waiting in line at the grocery store, he mentioned to the cashier that he had just moved and inquired about the friendliness of the people. She simply asked him how the people were in the town that he had just moved out of. He casually stated that they were the kindest folks around. Without batting an eyelash, the cashier said that the people in the new town were the same way as well. *In the final analysis, the way that we treat others becomes the standard by which we will be treated. Be kind to people and we suddenly find people going out of their way to be kind to us. Be respectful to people and we begin to notice how respectful people become toward us. What goes around eventually comes around.*

Some of us may be thinking that there are a few inner attitudes that may need some work. I think if we were all honest, we would see that there have been times where a certain attitude we held did more harm than good. Maybe there were moments in our life where we could have shown a little more kindness to a person. We may even remember a time where we were not as respectful as we should have been.

Some of us may be able to reflect upon undesirable moments where a bad attitude crept in and made relating to others more difficult. But these should not be looked upon as bad memories to bury away. If anything, these unpleasant experiences can become great learning tools in discovering what attitudes work and what do not work. It brings to mind the time someone asked Thomas Edison what he thought of the thousands of experiments that had failed prior to his discovery of electricity. He corrected the person by stating that the failed experiments were not failures but were successful in showing him thousands of ways that would not work.

Failure is only a failure if we fail to learn from it.

The mistakes of yesterday can be used for tomorrow's successes. Today is the first day of the rest of our life. It is not yesterday. It is fresh and new, *and what we do with it is up to us*. Starting this day we can begin to make positive changes in our attitudes. Whatever happened in the past is nothing but dusty pages of history. We can start today to make changes that will reflect such virtues as kindness, patience, and caring. It is never too late to "clean out the attic" and begin afresh.

Improving on all six attitudes

One of the first steps in making improvements in our attitude is to recognize the undesirable ones that we still cling to. Maybe we could be a little more kind to those we work with, or a bit more patient with our customers. It could be that we have lost showing others how much we appreciate them. Whatever attitude we identify as needing a makeover, we can start on the right path by simply acknowledging that improvement needs to take place in a certain attitude. Let's take a closer look at all six attitudes and discover a few ideals for improvement.

Improving our friendliness

I cannot think of a better way to improve in being friendlier to people than simply learning to greet others with a smile or a kind word. On the most part, people are generally reserved when they are around new people. The reason for this is that they are unfamiliar and do not know what to expect. Unlike familiar faces, being in the presence of strangers tends to make us slightly reserved. So what is the icebreaker that can help in these new situations that we will encounter from time to time? Is there something that we can do to connect to others without being overly intrusive? What behavior would be socially acceptable?

A smile is a language everyone understands.

A great solution to these situations is to simply express a friendly smile to those we meet for the first time. *This small gesture will work wonders in breaking down the walls of unfamiliarity and allowing trust to enter. When we show ourselves to be friendly, people tend to suddenly open up to us because they now sense that we can be trusted.* This is one of the benefits we receive when we are friendly. People begin to open up because they feel that we can be trusted. This especially works well with our customers. When a customer senses our welcoming attitude, they will begin to open up and trust that we will provide them with exceptional service.

Showing others that we are friendly is a goal that every dentistry customer service representative should strive for. This attitude alone can make the ultimate difference in how the customer will rate the service provided. When we consistently show others benevolence through our words and actions, they in turn will feel more comfortable in our presence. Improving on being friendlier can happen by simply taking small steps each day. *Maybe we can begin to practice smiling more. It could be that we need to work on our tone of voice. It can be as uncomplicated as being the first to greet others.* Whatever we may choose, the important point is that others begin to recognize that we are accommodating and approachable. One way to discover whether others find us friendly is by being aware of how they react to us. More than likely we will find people responding positively to our welcoming attitude. Remember,

What goes around eventually comes around.

Improving our enthusiasm

Enthusiasm awakens and inspires others to capture a renewed passion for living.

There is something about being in the presence of a person who is filled with enthusiasm. We sense their inner excitement and desire it in our own lives. People with a passion for life have a way of awakening others with inspiration and hope. Not only can it become contagious, but it also makes us want to capture a new zeal for living. If we look back on moments in our past, we can find periods of being enthused about waking up in the morning. Maybe it was caused by a new job or an exciting project that we were working on. Whatever the reason, we could not wait to jump out of bed and begin the day. It was as if we had renewed energy and an excitement that carried us throughout the day. It also seemed as if we needed less sleep. *(It reminds me of the few hours of sleep that Thomas Edison needed due to his enthusiasm for discovery.)* These are a few rewards that having an attitude of enthusiasm can bring to each of us.

But what happens when we have lost the zest for life? What can we do to improve on our lack of enthusiasm that we have succumbed too? Is there anything that we can do to recapture some passion that somewhere along the line escaped us? As mentioned earlier in the chapter on enthusiasm, the first and foremost way to recapture an attitude of enthusiasm is to see that life is truly a gift. Each moment is all we have. *We cannot live in the past and surely cannot live in the future. Life can only be lived moment by moment.* Out of this comes a renewed outlook on life. Enthusiasm soon follows.

Another way to improve on our attitude of enthusiasm is by pursuing a hobby or passion that is of interest to us. What exactly is it that makes you energized about life? Looking back in your own life, what activities or experiences made you excited to start the day? *I believe that one of the major obstacles that suffocate our enthusiasm is that we have simply forgotten what we once enjoyed.* Think of your childhood years. Surely there were hobbies and interests that would get you excited about waking up. Maybe it was collecting baseball cards or fishing at the local pond with your friends. Maybe reading adventure books brought enthusiasm into your life. It could have been setting up a lemonade stand for the neighborhood kids. Whatever the pursuit was, it is important to rediscover within yourself what captured your interest and made you jump out of bed in the morning.

I can recall many fond memories of activities that filled my young life with enthusiasm and unquenchable excitement. There was the time that my brothers and friends would play baseball everyday in the field next to our house. I can remember having lemonade stands and little carnivals in front of our house. I can even recapture the excitement of trying to build a wooden raft for the river that flowed in front of my grandmother's cottage. As I look back at these fond childhood memories, I can still feel the excitement that these experiences brought into my life. I can recall being excited about waking up in the morning so that I could start the new adventure that captured my attention and enthusiasm.

I share this for one simple reason. *Enthusiasm can come back into our lives when we learn to recapture the excitement of what youth once brought us. If we dig deep enough, I believe that every one of us had something that awoke our senses and made us feel more alive.* But what tends to happen as we become older? We enter our teen years and eventually finish our schooling only to be greeted with a job. Eventually we begin to take on more responsibilities that somehow make us forget about past hobbies and activities that once brought enthusiasm into our lives. Our adult life also brings new responsibilities. Life becomes preoccupied with a career and everyday tasks. Everything from paying the bills to taking our kids to practice begins to occupy our life. Nothing is wrong with these responsibilities. In fact, doing all of these things may bring us enthusiasm *(except maybe paying the bills!)* But the problem can arise when we have lost touch of the things that once grabbed our attention.

By looking deeper into the hobbies or activities that once captivated us, *we can soon discover that we may have forgotten what we truly use to enjoy doing.* Why is it that we suddenly quit fishing when it was such a part of our youth? Being able to dig up some worms with our friends and head off to a favorite fishing hole once played a big part in our childhood. We may even have daydreamed about being able to fish after school and couldn't wait for the bell to ring so we could head off to the pond. Somewhere along the way we simply stopped doing what truly made us feel enthused about living. It could have been reading or hiking in the backyard woods looking for different types of plants. Our goal now as adults is to rediscover the simple activities that once made us excited about waking up in the morning.

The reason that I am bringing us back to our childhood years is because children have such great imaginations and know how to have fun. *No other age group is better at showing us how to recapture enthusiasm and excitement*. They can teach us a lot about having fun and enjoying the simple pleasures of life. Watch them and they will lend a hand in helping us to remember past interests and hobbies that may have been sitting dormant for years.

Improving our caring

Have you ever met someone for the first time and walked away sensing something different about this person? In the short time after being introduced you immediately felt that they cared about people. There was something special in the way they communicated that left an indelible mark. Looking back, maybe it was how they listened intently as you spoke. They gave you the immediate impression that they were genuinely interested in what you had to say. There were no interruptions or trying to redirect the conversation back to them. *Because of this, you felt that this person actually cared about what you* had to say. *More importantly, you felt that this person cared about you.*

If we are to improve on developing an attitude of caring I am convinced that it must start with an improvement in our listening skills. As discussed in the earlier chapter on caring, when we truly listen to another person, it validates our sincere concern for them. Listening is one of the best gifts that we can give to another person. Whether it is a customer, co-worker, friend, or family member, our listening expresses to others that we care. On the other hand, a lack of listening expresses that we do not respect their thoughts and opinions.

The highest perfection we can obtain in the art of conversation is being able to listen intently and then respond appropriately.

Self-centeredness - Making every conversation revolve around me, myself, and I

Eventually people will begin to associate your name with someone who cares simply because you have taken the time to listen.

The power of listening is one of the key factors if we are to enrich our relationships with others. Let's take a look at one of the main reasons that we do not give another person the simple gift of listening. When our life revolves around the me, myself, and I syndrome, it becomes difficult to truly listen to another person. Every dialogue becomes an attempt to turn it in such a way as to have the conversation focus entirely on us. *The objective in conversing with others eventually becomes one-sided where we are only interested in sharing our opinions with little thought in what the other person may be saying.* Because of this, we simple cannot recognize our poor listening skills.

Recently I witnessed a conversation that will drive this point home. I was in a conversation with two people. During most of the conversation I simply sat and listened as they both talked. *All of a sudden it hit me that both people were talking to each other without actually listening to what the other person was saying.* When one person gave his opinion, the other would cut in as soon as there was a gasp for air and began giving his thoughts. Not one person asked a question or acknowledged what the other person had just shared. As I sat there, I could not help but notice that no one really wanted to listen but only to be heard.

If we are to convey that we care about others, maybe it is time to begin speaking less and listening more. *It is amazing how much we can learn if we will only stop long enough to pay attention to what others have to say.* I have thought about this quite often and have come to the conclusion that listening is much more beneficial. Listening allows us to learn more. It will also convey to others respect and a caring heart by giving them our undivided attention. There will be times when we will need to share and communicate. But in the vast majority of conversations, we should learn to honor others by intently listening to what they are saying.

A gossip talks to you about others; a bore talks to you about himself; and a brilliant conversationalist talks to you about you.

The real problem with selfishness is that it does not allow us to give others our undivided attention. This is because all of our attention is focused on us. *We see every conversation as an opportunity to chat about us and tell everything that is happening in our own life.* Without realizing it, every dialogue soon becomes one that revolves around our own opinions. We then force others to listen to us with no thought of their opinion. *In extreme cases, it can eventually come to a point where fewer and fewer people want to engage in a conversation with us simply because of our poor listening skills.* This inner selfishness also conveys that our opinion is really the only one that matters. This of course can become detrimental in expressing our concern for others.

If we are to improve in showing people that we care, it is essential that we give them the opportunity to speak. Learning to ask questions and really listen to what is being said will convey that the other person's opinions are important. One way of knowing whether a person is truly listening is by the amount of questions he or she will ask. If we take the time to observe a dialogue, we will discover that few people ask questions. This may be a reflection of poor listening skills. *But when we come across a person during a conversation that asks questions about what was just shared, be sure to mark this person as a keen listener. This is a sure sign that an excellent listener is in our presence.* Learn to listen and others will soon appreciate the consideration that you have shown them.

Improving our respect

*Give a person respect and instantly you will
bring out the best in them.*

The attitude of respect is important if we are to convey to others that we value them. This is essential whether we are serving a customer or conversing with a friend. *Showing respect has a way of bringing out the best in others. It makes people feel significance.* When we view others as important, then expressing to them our respect will only come naturally. This belief in seeing all people as significant is the key if we are to begin showing more respect.

Over the years I have had the privilege of becoming friends with people who are very respectful toward others. It did not matter who the other person was or the position held. Again and again these special friends showed respect. *Their secret is that they have never considered themselves to be any better than the next person. They simply view everyone as significant.* In the same manner, our goal should be similar. We will instantly improve in communicating respect to others if we view each person as important. And in the end, isn't everyone important?

The Story of Mr. Jones

Let me share a story of a person who had a gift of showing respect to everyone. Mr. Jones arrived earlier than expected and entered through the side doors where the 2,000 employees would always enter. It was the first day that he would arrive to the company where he would be the new president and CEO. Everyone knew that the new CEO would be arriving shortly, but had no idea what he looked like. As Mr. Jones walked through the building, he offered a friendly greeting to everyone he came across. As he continued walking he noticed that an employee was having a difficult time setting up long tables in a conference room. Without hesitation, Mr. Jones walked over, took off his coat, and lent a hand. Fifteen minutes later he was immensely thanked for helping with the tables and simply shook the man's hand and smiled.

As he continued walking, he noticed the cafeteria entrance and figured that he would have some breakfast before heading to the main office. As he ordered his breakfast at the front counter, he could not help but overhear people around him talking about the new CEO and wondering out loud what kind of person he would be. Smiling inside, he quietly picked up his order and began searching for an available table to sit at. After looking around for a minute, he noticed the same people who had previously been talking at the counter sitting at a table. He casually walked over and asked if he could join them. They smiled in return and gestured for him to sit down. Introducing himself simply as Jack, the people at the table continued to talk about the new CEO and spoke about the new improvements that they had hoped would happen when this new president arrived. They then turned to Mr. Jones and asked what he would like to see improved. Jack simply shared that he thought the ideas given were excellent. Not only did Mr. Jones show respect to everyone that he met, but he also listened well.

Upon leaving, he thanked them for allowing him to join them for breakfast and headed toward the main office. As he approached the front desk, he introduced himself and began meeting everyone in the office. After being introduced to the management staff, he was then given a tour of the building and informed that he would be introduced to the company employees in the large conference center. Upon arriving at the main center where everyone had gathered to meet the new CEO, Mr. Jones walked up to the podium. Imagine the surprised expressions of those who had previously met him without realizing that he was the new CEO. They could not get over the fact that he did not tell anyone that he was the new president. Just as impressive was the genuine kindness and respect that he had expressed to everyone that he had previously met. This company was indeed fortunate to have hired Mr. Jones.

The story could not end without sharing about Mr. Jones's best asset. From early in life, *Mr. Jones understood that you could always bring out the best in others if you simply gave them respect. This belief had stayed with Jack all of his life and was one of the main reasons why he had been successful in his career.* He believed that everyone was significant and should be given respect.

Improving our encouraging

If there is one attitude that will instantly help to lift others up, it is being an encourager. When we encourage people, it is as if we were lending a hand and giving them the confidence to move forward. Giving a kind and encouraging word to another person is not only a way to show that we want the best for them, but also that we care. *Reflect back and we will discover that those most influential in our lives have encouraged us and filled us with inspiration.* They had a way of lifting us up either by a kind word or a helping hand. Whether it was a coach, a teacher, or a leader, the people that we have been most fond of have motivated us to become our best. This is the power of encouragement.

I remember as a young boy going to the state playoffs with my hockey team. Arriving at the ice arena, I was handed a letter from one of the fathers who had a son on my team. It was a simple letter of encouragement informing me that I was a fine skater and needed to do the best that I could in this playoff game. This letter was given to me over thirty years ago and I still have fond memories of it. I do not remember much about the game, but I will always remember this letter that was given to me prior to the big game. This again shows the power of encouragement. In similar fashion, I coached my son's junior high basketball team this past year. It was a fun experience coaching these well-mannered kids. During our season-end banquet I decided to buy every boy a devotional book. On the first page of each book I wrote an encouraging letter to each boy and specifically shared how he had contributed to the team during the season. Like the letter I received years ago, I am almost certain that these young men will remember the encouraging words that were written to them.

If we are to improve in our attitude of encouragement, the first step we need to do is watch our words. By this I mean that we are to avoid making critical remarks. *Any form of gossip, slander, or discourteous words toward others should never be a part of our conversations.* The reason is because unkind words can affect our attitude. Without realizing it, we can begin to become more critical and lose our ability to encourage people. By making it a habit of building others up, we will soon discover that our attitude will also begin to change for the better.

Becoming a positive influence on others will happen when we make sincere encouragement a daily part of our lives. *Be a person who finds the best in others. By doing this, we will begin to overlook the petty imperfections that are a part of all of us.* When we live with a critical eye and look only for the blemishes in others, we will soon find that it becomes difficult to offer kind words. If we are to be more encouraging, the first step must be to find the positive qualities in others and overlook the minor flaws. By looking past these flaws, we will now be given the opportunity to see the uniqueness of each individual. This then allows us to see others in a more positive light.

Improving our Thankfulness

Joy is the result of a thankful heart.

I have discovered that the most contented people in life are the most thankful people. It is as if to say that the more thankful we are, the more content we become.

*Contentment comes as a result of living
a life of thankfulness.*

Thankfulness has a way of making our days more enjoyable and our life more fulfilling. When we live with appreciation, our whole world brightens up. We view everything in a different light. Being thankful positively affects every area of our life. From the way we view our friends to the meal sitting before us, having a grateful heart simply makes life better. No other attitude has a more profound effect on our level of happiness. Our life becomes filled with more joy and contentment because of this grateful attitude. We view life differently because of the thankfulness that resides within us.

Think about the people that we know who have a continual thankful outlook on life. *One common trait in these contented people is that they rarely complain about anything.* They tend to view everything differently. When others may quickly jump at the opportunity to grumble, these people will forfeit the chance to join in. It could be that they understand something that others may not be aware of. It also could be that they have discovered that complaining and grumbling eventually erode a thankful heart.

*Living with an attitude of thankfulness disappears
as soon as we start to complain.*

If we are to improve on our attitude of thankfulness, maybe it would be a good idea to learn from those who rarely complain. The first and most important lesson that we can discover and implement into our own lives is that grumbling only makes life worse. *The real problem with complaining is that it eventually takes root and begins to grow from bad to worse. It is as if complaining feeds on itself until one day our entire life becomes one big complaint.* Without realizing it, our outlook on everything becomes bleak and desolate. No longer can we enjoy the simple gift of life because of the irritable attitude that constant complaining brings. In the end, we should avoid all forms of complaining and grumbling if we want to maintain a thankful heart.

Chapter 10

Closing Thoughts

*Our highest and most privileged calling in life
is having the honor to serve others.*

As we close, I would like to thank you for arriving at this point in the book. I would also like to encourage each reader to take a personal inventory of the six attitudes that may need a tune-up from time to time. This periodic check-up will help each of us to live more fulfilled lives. Maybe it could be that we need a tune-up in the area of friendliness. Or maybe it is working on showing others that we care. It could be as simple as working on being more thankful. No matter what attitude may need adjusting, remember to take it a day at a time. I like to say that Rome was not built in a day. Remember to take small steps in making improvements. In no time, things will begin to look brighter. Your customers and friends will start to notice a more friendly and caring attitude and respond favorably.

*The quickest way to finish a task
is to begin it.*

My goal in writing *Dentistry Customer Service Superstars* was to hopefully give every reader an understanding of the importance of our attitudes and how they can help us to serve better. The attitudes that we live with will make all the difference in how we approach life. Each attitude will determine everything from how well we perform on the job to how rewarding our relationships are. Without a right outlook, our vision becomes blurry because of the subtle effects that a poor attitude can bring about. As an example, when we have lost the appreciation of life, nothing seems to satisfy us. When we have lost the trait of respecting others, we never quite feel respected. Or what if we decided to live with an unfriendly attitude? More than likely, we would begin noticing fewer friends in our life.

Life becomes more rewarding when we live with these six attitudes. By showing ourselves to be friendly, enthused, caring, respectful, encouraging, and thankful, not only will our service toward others instantly improve, but we will also find ourselves enjoying the gift of life on a much higher level. Remember,

Friendliness is the first judgment customers make.
Enthusiasm enhances the customer's experience.
Caring creates customer loyalty.
Respect conveys our willingness to serve.
Encouragement creates a positive environment.
Thankfulness conveys our sincere appreciation.

May your days be filled with the right attitudes.

Best Regards,

Cary Cavitt
Author, Speaker and Founder
Service Starts with a Smile Seminars ™
Visit us at: www.carycavitt.com

About the Author

Since 1975 Cary has personally served over 100,000 customers. During these years he has observed and learned what truly brings customers back. Cary's zeal to find out what customers want has been his driving passion in building a successful career as a Golf Professional.

After receiving a B.A. at the University of Michigan and an M.A. at Eastern Michigan University, Cary then went on to receive his PGA Membership and become an award-winning Head Professional at various clubs in the Midwest.

Cary's expertise is in the area of customer service. His first book, *Service Starts with a Smile,* focuses on sixty-nine reasons why customers return. In it Cary explores the real influences that determine whether a customer will return.

Because of Cary's vast experience in providing over 35 years of personal service to a wide variety of clients, he is well qualified to coach others in what customers are really looking for when they make contact with a business.

Outside of his enthusiasm for teaching others the real reasons that customers return, Cary enjoys time with his wife Carol and their three children, Sara, Nathan, and Hanna.

Service Starts with a Smile Seminars ™

Helping America Serve Better

We offer dentistry customer service seminars to fit your organizational needs for understanding how to create a great customer service experience. The insightful workshops are for both management and employees and are intended to build five-star service within your organization.

The Onsite *Service Starts with a Smile Seminars* ™ are available for the organization that is looking to improve on dentistry customer service. The fun and interactive presentation will motivate each team member to *want to serve customers more effectively.* Along with addressing why customers return, we will also explore *why customers choose not to return.*

If you are looking for a life-changing seminar of insightful applications for your organization, the onsite seminars may be exactly what you are looking for. The positive changes will be felt immediately!

More information can be found at:

www.carycavitt.com

Cary's first book, *Service Starts with a Smile* can be purchased at carycavittconsulting.com. In it Cary shares sixty-nine reasons why customers return. The insightful tips are great for those who would like to build a stronger service team and keep customers coming back time and again.

Five-Star Service focuses on what great service looks like and how to consistently do it. The book is broken down into sixteen questions pertaining to customer service. The answers are simple and to the point and are a great reference and reminder of what it takes to bring about five-star service to our customers.

In *Winning the Customer,* service expert Cary Cavitt helps us to understand the seventeen needs of the customer. Every customer is measuring how they are being treated. Everything from how happy we are to serve them to making them feel accepted will ultimately determine whether or not they become loyal.

Healthy relationships result when we develop healthy inner qualities. In *People Skills* we will learn that the more inner virtues we possess, the better our relationships will be. We will also find our relationships improving as we begin to build the sixty-five qualities into our lives. In the end, we will discover that positive changes start on the inside.

In his insightful way of shedding light on the art of service, Author and Speaker Cary Cavitt looks at what it really takes to deliver exceptional service. Great service can only happen when we serve with the *five mindsets* discussed. Whether your establishment is an exclusive resort on an island or a local business in your community, *Luxury Service* will show you how to create service that goes above and beyond what your client expected.

www.ingramcontent.com/pod-product-compliance
Lightning Source LLC
Chambersburg PA
CBHW071440180526
45170CB00001B/401